WILDBLUE I
TRUE CRIME
features

KEVIN SULLIVAN
KENTUCKY
BLOODBATH

Ten Bizarre Tales Of Murder
from the Bluegrass State

WILDBLUE
PRESS

WildBluePress.com

KENTUCKY BLOODBATH published by:
WILDBLUE PRESS
1153 Bergen Pkwy Ste I #114
Evergreen, Colorado 80439

WILDBLUE PRESS is registered at the U.S. Patent and
Trademark Offices.

978-1-942266-17-4 Mass Market Paperback ISBN
978-1-942266-16-7eBook ISBN

Interior Formatting/Cover Design by Elijah Toten
www.totencreative.com

Art Director Carla Torrisi Jackson

Editor Tom Panholzer
(tpanholzer@yahoo.com)

Other WildBlue Press Books
By Kevin Sullivan

VAMPIRE: *The Richard Chase Murders*
http://wbp.bz/vampire

THE TRAIL OF TED BUNDY:
Digging Up The Untold Stories
http://wbp.bz/trailbundy

THE BUNDY SECRETS: *Hidden Files*
On America's Worst Serial Killer
http://wbp.bz/bundysecrets

Contents

Death by Sword

Twenty-two-year-old Carol Frances Mudd reported to work at the Stone Castle Museum in Bardstown, Kentucky like usual that mild November morning in 1982. It was the day after Halloween, but that would not have been on her mind as she prepared to receive those wishing to see the museum's fine collection of miniature toy soldiers and antique weapons. For Carol, it probably felt like just another day at work. But today would be unlike any previous day in her brief life. Today, Carol Mudd would be savagely murdered.

At approximately 1:30 p.m., as postman Charles Meredith was passing in front of the Stone Castle while delivering the mail, he saw a man, later identified as Anthony Russell Gowin, talking to a woman about a whiskey barrel. Stopping for a moment, a brief conversation ensued among the three, and twenty-year-old Tony Gowin told Meredith he'd been inside the museum, but no one was there. Meredith later told police that Gowin then left and he "did not seem to be in a hurry."

At around 2 p.m., teenage brothers Bill and Joe Pheiffer stopped by the museum to view the exhibits and browse the bookstore. "I went in," remembered Bill Pheiffer, "and I thumbed through the books… and when I went in there, it kind of struck us that the place was empty…we didn't hear anybody upstairs, and we didn't hear anybody downstairs." Over the next few minutes, the Pheiffer brothers milled about the first floor. While Bill spent time in the bookstore, Joe looked over the exhibits. They didn't hear anyone else moving around in any of the rooms, nor did they venture upstairs. Once Bill had selected a book he wanted to purchase, he stood at the cash register like a sentry, perhaps believing such an action would be sure to produce an employee. But as the minutes passed with no one entering the room, Bill asked his brother if he'd run upstairs and see if anyone was there. "So he ran up…," Bill said, "and I heard him going across the floor…and I waited near the cash register. I didn't hear anybody talking up there, so I assumed that he hadn't seen anybody really. So he came downstairs, and he told me that he'd seen something on the floor that scared him." Upon hearing this, both boys climbed the steps for a better look, but at the time, Bill Pheiffer told the police, he didn't believe it was anything serious.

Once the brothers were upstairs they passed through first one room and entered another that contained a large diorama. As Bill turned to look over at the table displaying the diorama, Joe interrupted him and said, "No, not here. It's in here!" Bill Pheiffer then glanced in the direction his brother was pointing and saw what had frightened him. "I saw the midsection of the body, and I really didn't know what it was...I'd seen dummies before, and it looked like a dummy" Although the blood looked fresh to the brothers, they believed it was some kind of fake, or a prop of sorts, because her neck and hands were as "white as can be." It wasn't until he looked closely at the face did he recognize it as the woman he'd seen there previously. To his horror, he knew he was looking at an actual dead body.

Protruding from the top of her neck was a three-foot medieval broadsword, which had been removed from one of the museum exhibits nearby. Apparently, death came quickly, as the sword "had been thrust into the base of the neck down through the soft tissue around the heart, into her left lung, and severing the aorta thus causing her death." As one might expect, there were numerous injuries to the body prior to death, including: "multiple head injuries from a beating with a blunt object...a pattern of bruising consistent with a shoe print (found) on the victim's neck...lacerations to the left hand and fingers..." After Mudd was dead, her killer twice drove a dagger into her chest. (Court records contained the phrase "buried to the hilt" when referring to this.) And there were several cuts made to the face and neck.

Between 6 p.m. and 7 p.m. that evening, Gowin telephoned Donald Miller and asked if he wanted to come over and play guitar. A short time later, Miller's mother dropped him off at the Gowin residence and for a time, the two young men passed the time playing their instruments. Afterward, (Miller later told police), Gowin showed him his sword, and Miller let him see a knife he'd purchased just that day. Soon, the two went outside where Gowin proceeded to demonstrate his prowess with a sword.

After placing a cardboard box on a saw horse, Gowin began his exhibition by first facing his target: "He swung (the sword) one way and he'd spin around and...make nicks...he made nicks in the card board box and then he had his back turned to the...box." Without looking, Gowin thrust the sword under one arm, striking the box squarely in the middle where he had previously placed an X. Indeed, Gowin's movements were so fast, Miller believed he might actually injure himself before it was all over. But Miller's fears were quickly erased as Gowin spun back around, and in a series of very quick movements, "slashed the box all to pieces."

Tony Gowin's next door neighbor, Kentucky State Police Trooper Steve Campbell, had witnessed Gowin doing this on several occasions, and had watched him "go into the back yard and take a machete and chop a card board box into shreds." Campbell also considered Gowin to be a very strange individual, and perhaps even dangerous.

After Miller and Gowin went back inside the house, Miller asked if he'd heard about "the girl that got killed?" Miller said that as soon as he uttered these words, Gowin got a puzzled look on his face and may have become slightly irritated. After responding with a simple "No," Gowin stood up and told Miller he was going upstairs, Miller assumed, to talk to his parents. Within minutes, Gowin and his stepfather walked next door to speak with Trooper Campbell and Mrs. Gowin came into the room to sit with young Miller.

Evidently, Gowin had gone next door to tell Campbell he'd been to the Stone Castle that day but had not seen anyone while there. Upon hearing this, Campbell asked if he could have the clothes he'd worn at the museum, and Gowin said yes. Later, as he turned the clothes over to the police, he mentioned he'd washed them sometime after returning home from the museum.

Before Gowin left that evening, Campbell told him he would need to meet with detectives for a more formal interview tomorrow, and Gowin agreed. Miller said after Gowin returned home from Officer Campbell's house, he seemed relieved. He also mentioned that, before leaving that night, he watched him put something in his car; he believed under the driver's seat, but in the darkness he couldn't see what Gowin was carrying in his hand.

On November 2, Gowin met with authorities at the Stone Castle museum. Present were Detective Ted Hettel, Officer Steve Campbell, and Lieutenant Edwards. At the meeting, Gowin admitted being at the museum yesterday, but said he hadn't seen anyone. According to Gowin, he entered the museum and found it silent and empty. After calling out three or four times and receiving no response, he visited the exhibits on the bottom floor and left. It was at this time that he saw the postman, Charles Meredith. What the police knew –but Gowin didn't- was that before Carol was killed, she recorded in a logbook the receiving of one customer.

As Tony Gowin was the only person known to have been at the museum (except for the Pheiffer brothers who discovered the body) Gowin must have been considered a suspect, at least one of several. Yet, because Gowin's fingerprints were not found on the sword or any other pertinent objects dusted by police, and perhaps because the foot print bruise left on Carol's neck was between a size 7½ to an 8 and Gowin's shoe size was an 8½ D, he remained only a suspect.

Indeed, two and one half years would pass before police would even get close to making an arrest. Perhaps, even Carol Mudd's killer believed he'd gotten away with it. But the final chapter in this case had not yet been written.

In May 1985, Kentucky State Police Detective Robert Foster became actively involved in the Carol Mudd murder investigation. After reviewing the file, Foster became very interested in Tony Gowin due to his fascination with the game Dungeons and Dragons, the occult, his interest in the martial arts, and his known skill with edged weapons, particularly swords.

Once detectives began looking closely into Gowin's background, it became clear the investigation was going in one direction only: straight toward Tony

Gowin. And what emerged at this time was a very disturbing picture in which each person interviewed revealed very similar and shocking things to authorities. One individual, the mother of one of Gowin's friends, said even as a child, Tony Gowin loved "Bloody, weird movies where people get their heads chopped off." She also spoke of many emotional problems, and how she believed he was "emotionally disturbed." Rosemary Lawrence, a former girlfriend of Gowin, told police that "Gowin was a very weird individual, that he was considered weird by all the people around him." Lawrence also said Gowin was a member "of the Black Cult, which is devil worshipping."

When police arrived at the home of Jeannette Marie Bowling, who had dated Gowin during the time of the murder, she asked if they were "interested in Tony Gowin because of the Mudd murder?" According to police, "Miss Bowling dated Gowin during the time of the murder and she stated that she thought Gowin was the murderer from the very beginning. She stated Gowin would be considered a dangerous person, a fanatic about knives and karate, and that he had hang-ups on sex."

Bowling also said that when she heard about the murder, she told her family she believed "Tony had killed the girl in Bardstown." She declared to detectives that Gowin was a drug user, and he had "dual personalities." When the officers asked Bowling to elaborate on Gowin's sexual hang-ups, she declined. Still, they would hear all about them from a Carla Nalley, who had been Gowin's

11

girlfriend perhaps a year or more before Carol Mudd was killed.

According to Nalley, Gowin liked rough sex, and it was important for him, at least during intercourse, to pretend he was someone else: a doctor, soldier, or someone with authority, and sometimes he would pretend to rape her while holding an imaginary knife to her throat. She also mentioned his personality could change from good to bad very quickly: "One minute he would be a very kind and considerate person. The next minute he would be talking about killing somebody or cutting somebody's head off."

Meanwhile, Tony Gowin, who'd enlisted in the Marine Corps one year after the murder, was fighting drug and alcohol problems and was in fact in the process of being driven out of the service. The following is from a report dated June 18, 1985, from the Naval Alcohol Rehabilitation Center, Naval Air Station, in Jacksonville, Florida:

"Progress in treatment was satisfactory until the 5th week of treatment "when the patient voluntarily disclosed that he had used marijuana during the treatment period. On 5 June 1985, it was determined that the patient was non –amenable to treatment for alcoholism and drug abuse. He was dropped from treatment and returned to his command with a recommendation that he be administratively separated from the United States Marine Corps."

Four days earlier, on June 14, Kentucky State Police contacted the U.S.Naval Investigative Service with information concerning Gowin, and warrants were issued for his arrest. Ten days later, detectives Robert Foster and Bruce Slack arrived at Camp Lejeune, North Carolina, and along with a person from the Naval Investigative Service, transported Gowin to the Naval Intelligence building, and read him his rights.

That same afternoon, personal items of Gowin's seized by the authorities included the satanic bible, books on satanic rituals, witchcraft, Dungeons and Dragons, as well as various notebooks containing satanic writing and drawings. All of these pieces were released to detectives Foster and Slack, and by 12 p.m., on June 29, Anthony R. Gowin was on his way back to Kentucky. "Keeping in mind," wrote Detective Foster in his report, "that Tony Gowin had declined to make any further statements without consulting an attorney, the conversation on the trip home was of a general nature, with no attempt made to interrogate Mr. Gowin. After being several hours into our trip home, out of the clear blue sky, Tony Gowin made a spontaneous, voluntary statement that he felt as though he needed some professional help. He informed us that it is possible that he could have killed Carol Mudd, however, he does not remember it."

Gowin also admitted talking with Mudd that day – something he denied during his first interview - but said he went "blank" during the conversation and could only remember running from the museum, feeling nauseous, and experiencing a loud roaring in his head. Gowin also told the detectives he had taken

13

two Quaaludes that morning.

Back in Kentucky, Gowin was placed in the Hardin County Jail. On July 3, Foster and Slack transported him to the Nelson County courthouse for his arraignment. Of course, no bond was set due to the nature of the charges against him and the belief that he would flee the state if given the chance. Once his arraignment was complete, he was returned to jail. On the return trip however, Foster and Slack again advised him of his rights and then began asking about the statements he had made on the trip from Camp Lejeune on his way back to Kentucky. Gowin again repeated the story of talking with Mudd, going blank, and leaving the museum feeling sick and scared with the roaring in his head; a roaring he said sounded much like that of a lawn mower. Gowin added that when he saw the postman, he believed Meredith was a threat and that he felt like hitting him. He also said that after he returned home, he walked around for several hours before calming down.

Tony Gowin would make the same confession at least two more times before the trial, and his statements about going blank, the roaring in his head, and the possibility of killing Carol Mudd, were always the same. However, his later statements contained information about his involvement with Satanism, and a second personality, a person referred to as "Anthony Russell," and how this other personality would take over whenever he became angry.

Although much evidence was presented at Gowin's trial, the prosecution submitted one piece of evidence they likened to a type of calling-card left by the killer. Found on Carol Mudd's body was the rear part of a pin attachment, the part that holds the needle in place once it's been pressed through the clothes and was obviously attached to the main body of an unknown object.

As luck would have it, however, this piece was later matched up with a satanic star found in the pocket of one of Gowin's jackets when the police searched his home in Bardstown. The star has two inverted crosses on the front and the anti-Christ number, 666. The rear of the star contains a small gold broadsword. Both the broadsword and the pin attachment found on Carol Mudd have broken weld spots, and when these two pieces were examined by William McBrayer of the Kentucky State Police Crime Laboratory, using a stereo microscope, the match was perfect. McBrayer testified that by using his "ten point comparison" he could "state without a doubt, that the sword and pin back had been attached to each other."

Although Gowin's attorney presented his own expert witness who disputed McBrayer's findings, it would make little difference to the jury who considered the circumstantial evidence against Gowin overwhelming. On April 14, 1986, Tony Gowin was convicted of the murder of Carol Frances Mudd and received a sentence of thirty years. Almost one year later, on March 12, 1987, the Kentucky Supreme Court upheld the decision of the lower court, leaving the family of Carol Mudd, and most of the residents of Bardstown, relieved Gowin was going to prison for a very long time.

Four months after the Stone Castle murder, Gowin composed a song which he titled "The Hunter." This, along with other of his writings and drawings, was discovered during the search of his Bardstown residence. The lyrics to this particular song were presented to the jury so they could view for themselves the mind of Tony Gowin. The following is taken from the closing of the song:

"I've been waiting for you

For 10,000 years

Come to me pretty baby

Let me dry your tears

I promise just one pain you'll feel

Put your little hand in mine-

Feel my touch of steel"

In the years following her November 1982 murder, the grave of Carol Mudd has remained undisturbed. Only once, in November of 1984, did someone remove a commemorative plaque from her grave. Perhaps believing there was a connection, Detective Foster noted in his investigative report that Anthony Gowin was home on leave from the Marine Corps the same month the plaque disappeared.

The commemorative plaque has never been recovered.

BLOOD IN THE MOONLIGHT

At 8:00 p.m. on Friday, December 9, 1983, Albert and Mabel Bauer, both sixty-three, arrived at the Moose lodge in Louisville, Kentucky, for the annual Fraternal Order of Police dinner. For the past six years, Albert had been a deputy sheriff with the department and was apparently well liked. Those who saw the Bauers that evening said they seemed to be having a very good time, and they did not leave the party until 11:30 p.m.

The Bauer's only child, twenty-nine-year-old Albert Joseph Bauer Jr., had recently moved back into his parents' home. And Mabel Bauer was overheard at the dinner party saying that Jay, as he was affectionately referred to by family and friends, would soon be attending Sullivan Business College where he would hopefully "get straightened out." According to police records, young Albert Bauer had been arrested numerous times over the past few years, with charges ranging from disorderly conduct and drunken driving, to possession of illegal drugs. All of this was causing a financial strain on the family, but it is not known whether this was the reason Albert Bauer left his home in the first place. What is known, however, is that visits from their son would sometimes lead to shouts and arguments, according to their next door neighbor.

And while the Bauers were not the kind of people to discuss family problems with outsiders, Albert Sr. did mention to a coworker that he had in fact once "scuffled" with his son and in the past, drugs had been a problem with Jay. But tonight would not be the time to dwell on such things. Captain Joseph Lynch remembered seeing the Bauers as they were leaving the Moose lodge that night and even assisted Albert in backing his car out of the parking lot. Earlier in the evening, Lynch had accidentally spilled beer on Bauer's shoes, and Bauer and his friend had a good laugh about it. Sadly, that would be their last meeting.

At approximately 10:30 p.m., young Bauer entered Rick's Night Spot, a bar located on Poplar Level Road. Working the door that night was Ron Thomas, a thirty-four-year-old African-American who had known Bauer for several years and considered him a friend. Indeed, Thomas had helped Bauer move his furniture back into his parents' home. But tonight, things were different, and Thomas could see that Bauer was depressed. During the course of the evening Bauer sat by himself, first at the bar and then at a table. At one point, as Thomas was passing by, he noticed Bauer had his legs crossed, and so, as a joke, he flipped one leg off the other, fully expecting him to laugh and get him in a better mood. Instead of laughing, however, Bauer blurted out, "Don't do that again or I'll blow your black ass away!" Thomas couldn't see whether Bauer had a handgun, but he knew he was acting strangely and decided to leave him alone.

At 12:45 a.m., Bauer left Rick's Night Spot, and at 2:30 a.m., Louisville Police received the following call from Albert Bauer Jr.

"Louisville Police, Ms. Dempsey."

"Yes, there's been a murder."

"What happened…Where?"

"2609 Fordyce Lane."

"What happened?"

"I don't know."

"(Inaudible) my dad was…my dad was choked with…with a…with a necktie."

"Who choked him?"

"I don't know."

"Where are you, sir?"

"I'm at the address now."

"You're at the address now, and they're both there now?"

"Yes."

And then Bauer added, "One person's been stabbed. One person's been strangled."

Police and Emergency Medical Services were immediately dispatched to the scene.

The first person to arrive at the Bauer residence was Officer Jack Kendrick, a nine-year veteran of the Louisville Police Department. As soon as he parked his cruiser in front of the house, he noticed a man walking down the driveway toward him. There were no outside lights turned on, and in the moonlight it appeared that his clothes were wet, as if he'd been splashed with water. But upon closer examination, Kendrick could see that he was covered in blood, and he appeared to be high or intoxicated. Without hesitation, Albert Bauer identified himself and began repeating to Officer Kendrick what he'd told the dispatcher - that his parents had been murdered. This time, however, he became confused as to who had been stabbed and who had been strangled, and it was at this time that Kendrick looked down and noticed the cuts on Bauer's hands.

As Bauer led the officer to the side door where they entered the house through the kitchen, Kendrick asked if he knew who'd done this, and Bauer said, "No." Just before stepping inside the home, Kendrick radioed the E.M.S. (Emergency Medical Services) unit, telling them to continue on to this address - code 3 - and that homicide units should be sent as well.

Detectives Dene Ashcraft and Patrick Sowers of the homicide division were racing toward Fordyce Lane within minutes of the call, and Detective Michael Wohl, also of homicide, heard the report over his car radio and headed toward the scene as well. Having notified dispatch, Kendrick then drew his weapon and entered a nightmare.

Once inside the home, Kendrick saw the body of Mabel Bauer lying in a large pool of blood. Albert Bauer said he'd removed a pair of pinking shears from her body, and his father, who was lying dead in another part of the house, was a deputy sheriff. Before searching the rest of the house, Kendrick made Bauer sit in a chair in the dining room, which is situated next to the kitchen. He was doing this not only for Bauer's safety, but also his own. After all, he was walking through a home were a double homicide had just occurred, and there were yet no clear answers as to who committed the crime, or if anyone was even still inside the house.

Stepping out of the kitchen into the main hallway, Kendrick could see a pair of feet sticking out of a room, later identified as the living room. The feet, of course, belonged to Albert Bauer Sr., whose body was sprawled face up on the living room carpet, very close to the front door. From the position of the body, it appeared he was trying to escape through the front entrance when he was overtaken and killed.

During Kendrick's search of the premises, he received a call on his hand-held radio from Detective Ashcraft, asking if the homicides were inside or outside the house. When Kendrick told him the bodies were inside, Ashcraft asked him to secure the area, which he did. Although Detectives Ashcraft and Sowers would arrive only minutes after this call – and Detective Wohl only a minute or so later - Kendrick would later say, in such instances time seems to slow down and one minute can feel like ten.

From the moment detectives first entered the house they knew that almost every room "would be pertinent to the scene." As such, it was determined Detective Wohl would handle the upstairs and the body investigation, while Detective Ashcraft would look for evidence in the basement and outside the Bauer home. Meanwhile, Detective Sowers would escort Bauer downtown to the homicide office for questioning and to be photographed.

As officers began the tough work within the blood-spattered home, Bauer was being treated in the ambulance for the cuts on his hands. According to police, when E.M.S first entered the house, they checked Mr. and Mrs. Bauer for a pulse, but found none. Being mindful of what the police were doing, and not wishing to disturb any evidence, they very carefully raised the eyelids of the victims, exposing their flat and dilated pupils. Only then did they turn their attention to the strange and bloody young man.

It was at this time when one of the E.M.S technicians approached Bauer, and that she "could observe that he had lacerations to his hands" which, after closer observation, looked more like tears. Bauer also kept asking who was dead in the house, she said, and then he began saying there were, "knives and forks sticking out of her." As soon as his hands were bandaged, he was turned back over to Detective Sowers.

When Wohl began the body investigation, he started in the kitchen, where he found Mabel Bauer "lying in a massive pool of blood." Indeed, there was so much blood and the body in such a bad state, Wohl noted, "I will be unable to detail all of the injuries at this time. I will however note the more prominent indications of trauma."

There were eight puncture wounds in the upper left chest area, "and are paired...approximately 5/8" apart." When she was attacked, she was wearing pajamas – both top and bottom – which were now torn and slashed. There were numerous stab wounds to her back, as well as cuts and lacerations on her arms, hands, and various parts of her body. But whoever killed Mabel Bauer was not content with this alone. Whoever killed Mabel Bauer was filled with such rage that her throat had been sliced over and over again from ear to ear, and extensive cutting had occurred to the back of her neck leaving her almost completely decapitated. As far as the investigators were concerned, this wasn't the work of a burglar; this was the work of someone close to them.

As Wohl rolled the victim over to one side and away "from the south portion of the kitchen counter, which contains the stove and oven, there is noted to be a bent stainless steel kitchen type butcher knife, and also a long wooden handled butcher knife which is unbent. There are, additionally, a pair of unbroken eyeglasses, and also a two-pronged, wooden handled fork, which is bent almost double back, and a stainless steel paring knife, with the blade bent just above the juncture point of the handle." Wohl also noted the body was still warm with no sign of rigor mortis present. Because human hair was observed under the fingernails, the hands were covered with plastic bags before removal of the body from the home.

Like his wife, Albert Bauer Sr. was found lying on his back. He was clutching in his right hand a bloody, white bath towel. Lying across his chest was a necktie, the ends of which were still around the back of his neck. His eyes were partially open, and another white towel had been folded, or crumpled up underneath his neck. He, too, was warm to the touch, with no sign of rigor. Unlike his wife, however, he had not been stabbed to death, but severely beaten and strangled. "There is a good deal of blood splattered on the wall closest to the body and on the front door. Even so, blood spatter can be seen across the room on the opposite wall where a broken - or fragmented - piece of Mr. Bauer's dental plate was found near a closet door," the detective noted.

Of course, it was impossible for detectives to ascertain in what order the Bauer's had been attacked, or who was killed first. It is quite possible one victim was rendered unconscious very quickly, leaving plenty of time to commit the first murder, before returning to kill the first victim. Because of the blood spatter evidence, it was clear they had fought their attacker in several rooms of the house, and the initial struggle may have started in the basement where the son was living.

Entrance into the basement is gained through the kitchen, and the door leading to the stairwell was observed by Kendrick to be open when he first entered the house. As Ashcraft began his investigation of the basement, he noticed blood smears were present on both exterior and interior portions of the door and door knobs. "Entering into the stairwell and traveling in a westerly direction down the steps, the undersigned can observe that there are blood smears present on both the north and south walls. Several of these blood smears appear to be carried by a human hand, being as the smears are in a pattern, apparently caused by fingers dragging in a downward motion to the floor...a banister is observed situated along the north wall of the stairwell and extends to the bottom of the steps. There are several long smears of blood present on the banister railing, as if someone was holding onto the railing as they drug (sic) their hands up or down the rail."

The stairs are covered in a green tweed carpet, and Ashcraft quickly found blood spatters on the first, second, and third steps, with additional spatters on the sixth step along the edge. The seventh step had blood drippings, and the ninth step had a smear, possibly caused when someone fell. A good portion of the basement had been finished and is covered in the same green tweed carpet, and an unfinished area can be entered through a door to the left of the stairs. It was in this unfinished area where Detective Ashcraft found the furniture and personal items of Albert Bauer Jr.; although other items belonging to the son could be found throughout the entire basement area.

Upon close examination of a chest of drawers, Ashcraft found blood smears that apparently were going in a downward motion, "…and there are several human hairs in excess of two inches in length present on the front of the chest of drawers…" Directly in front of the chest was a large pool of blood which had not yet coagulated, and another, smaller pool of blood, just one foot from the steps. Blood smears were also observed on Bauer's bed, and the pillows contained blood spatters as well. Nearby was found a spiral notebook with a logo on the front that said *Sullivan Business College,* the same school Mabel Bauer had mentioned to a friend at the dinner party only hours earlier. Found next to the school binder was a religious paper with the title: *Safe in God's Keeping.* Blood spatters were also on this pamphlet.

It was clear to Ashcraft that an intense struggle occurred here, and no doubt included Albert Bauer Sr. Lying on the floor near the bed, Ashcraft recovered a heavy pewter mug covered in blood. Bending down to get a better look, he was able to see "what appears to be human head hairs present along the top edge of the mug." Shortly after the mug was found, the investigator had the hairs removed and bagged for testing, and carried the mug upstairs for comparison with the shape and size of a bruise found on Albert Bauer Sr., and it turned out being a perfect match.

It should also be noted that several bullets, or bullet fragments, from a .38 caliber revolver were found in various parts of the house. Although neither victim had been shot, the pistol was found lying next to the body of Mr. Bauer, and the trigger guard had been bent inward. Evidently, Mr. Bauer had been beaten with the pistol with such force the steel trigger guard was severely disfigured. When found, the gun was still in a "cocked" position, meaning the hammer had been pulled back and was ready to fire at the slightest squeeze of the trigger.

Because the son had stated in a rambling and contradictory manner that the killing of his parents were the result of two men, a K-9 unit was sent to the Bauer home to pick up any scents left behind by the pair. When Officer Larry Clopton arrived with his dog, he was told the intruders were supposed to have left through a basement window, which was now broken. Because of dew covering the grass, footsteps could be seen leading from the window to the privacy fence separating the Bauer residence from their neighbor at 2611 Fordyce Lane, and detectives wanted to know where the trail would lead.

Before removing his dog from the car, Officer Clopton asked everyone to move completely away from the scene, so that his dog could work unhindered. Everyone complied, and as soon as the German Shepherd was turned loose, he began to track; first from the basement window to the privacy fence, then around areas to the side of the Bauer home, and finally back to the car port and the side door leading back in to the kitchen. Clopton ran his dog twice around the house, both times resulted in the same conclusion: whoever left through the basement window went back into the house through the side door.

For the detectives, the results of the K-9 unit merely confirmed what they already believed. There was no burglary: The Bauers had been murdered by their only son. From the moment these seasoned detectives entered the house, they knew these killings were not the result of a botched robbery. Such carnage as they were forced to step over does not occur under such circumstances. True, a person can be killed in such an encounter, but the intruder will never stay around long enough to do what was done here. What was at work here was rage, pure and simple.

After discussing the situation, the investigators decided not to charge Bauer with murder without first obtaining the crime lab the results of the fingerprints and blood analysis recovered from the scene. Of course, there was little to no doubt in their minds who had killed the elderly couple, but they didn't want to do anything that would jeopardize their case once it came to trial. Instead, they decided to charge Albert Bauer with possession of a controlled substance, because of the handful of Quaaludes found among his personal items in the basement of his home. Once the results of the tests from the lab were received, he would be charged with murder.

After Bauer was officially arrested - and only minutes before he was transferred to the jail - Detective Ashcraft spoke with Bauer's attorney, Michael Green. During their conversation, Green made it clear he wanted his client out on bail as soon as possible. Ashcraft told him it was his intention to seek a high bond, seeing that Mr. Bauer is the principal suspect in a double homicide. Even so, Green was adamant, he would seek bail for his client, and if successful, he would notify them where Bauer was "being housed." Green also informed him he wanted to make a report on some missing items of Mrs. Bauer: The first, a gold clustered ring she normally wore on her wedding finger, and a braided gold necklace she'd borrowed for the sheriff's dinner.

As disappointing as it must have been for detectives, Judge John K. Carter was unable to grant their wish for a high bond due to the nature of the charge against Bauer. Had Bauer been charged with murder that would have been a different story, with different results, but a drug offense was simply not enough to hold him, and so, Albert Bauer was released on a thousand-dollar, full cash bond sometime before midnight Saturday.

True to his word, Michael Green phoned investigators with the news he had placed Albert Bauer in Room 2021 at the Galt House Hotel in downtown Louisville. After Mr. Green said goodbye to his client that evening, Bauer locked the door with the dead bolt and slid the security chain across the door as well. It was now early Sunday morning, and it appears Albert Bauer Jr. spent all of Sunday in seclusion at the hotel. However, at some point before going to bed Sunday night, Bauer left a wakeup call with the front desk for 7:30 a.m.

At 3:45 a.m., Diane Downs, an assistant supervisor of house cleaning at the Galt House, reported she'd heard dripping in the Archibald Room on the third floor, and because the room was dark and in a secluded area of the hotel, she decided not to go into the room without a member of management. A short time later, at approximately 4 a.m., she returned with the nighttime head of security, a Mr. Paul Ladd. When the lights were turned on, both Ladd and Downs could see where the water was pooling on the carpet, but it was too dark to see the area of the ceiling from which the leak was originating. After a few minutes, Ladd returned with a flashlight and shined it toward the leak. But instead of seeing just a simple roof problem, they were shocked by the sight of two human feet protruding from the ceiling. Upon seeing this, Downs became hysterical and ran out of the room screaming. Ladd immediately called police.

When Detectives Ashcraft and Sowers arrived, uniformed officers were already at the scene. So too were E.M.S. and members of the Louisville Fire Department, who helped remove the body from the roof of the ballroom. Ashcraft would later remark that as he and Sowers were leaving the homicide office after receiving the call, they could see the Galt House in the distance. A curtain was flapping in the breeze through a broken window, and he believed it was on the twentieth floor of the building. Of course, they figured Bauer was the jumper.

Once the wedged body was removed from the ceiling, detectives identified the body of Albert Joseph Bauer Jr. Wearing only a pair of jeans and a belt, Bauer had drifted some forty feet to the south of the window before impacting the third floor roof. Apparently, his was a controlled fall, wherein he was able to land on his feet. Detective Jeff Moody later said, Bauer's body was "...twisted. The legs cramped. The head is twisted back. There are severe injuries to feet, arms, buttocks, and possible head injuries." Ashcraft and Sowers were given permission by Paul Ladd to break the security on Room 2021.

Everything inside the room - except for the broken window - looked normal, and it was quickly determined that Bauer did not leave a note. Before leaving the room, Ashcraft phoned Michael Green and told him of Bauer's suicide. He also asked the attorney to telephone members of Bauer's family and let them know.

On December 16, 1983, after receiving the results from the crime lab, Albert Bauer Jr. was posthumously charged with the murder of his parents.

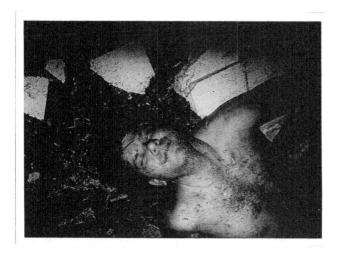

The body of Albert Bauer after being removed from the Galt House first floor ceiling

Albert Bauer Jr., having jumped out of a window twenty stories above, died on impact.

The home of Albert and Mabel Bauer, and their killer, Albert Jr.

RAMPAGE

On the afternoon of October 1, 1973, as forty-two-
year-old Geraldine Ewalt was waiting to pick up her
daughter at the Sayre School in downtown Lexington,
Kentucky, everything appeared to be normal. As she
sat in her car, others were also waiting in their cars
for their children to emerge after the final bell, just as
they had done every day since the school year began.
But today, the Sayre School, indeed, all of Lexington,
would be shaken by a brief but unexpected reign of
terror.

Situated directly across from Sayre was the federal
building, with the third floor being used as the
holdover for prisoners awaiting trial on federal
charges, and at 3:55 p.m., several men were seen
walking on the roof of the building's loading dock.
Two Metropolitan Police Department meter maids,
Gail Chasteen and Evelyn Green, at first believed
the men to be workers making repairs, but a man
standing nearby said they'd jumped from the third
floor window, as indeed they had, having feverishly

sawed through the window bars only moments before.

Just then, one of the men, thirty-three-year-old Wilmer Elvis Scott, a native of Tennessee with a long criminal record, jumped off the roof onto a grassy embankment and immediately got back up on his feet. Later, Scott would describe the incident to authorities: "I couldn't get off the roof. I kept walkin' around and everybody was lookin', people and a couple of Marshalls pulled in and people were starin' from across the street…so I just backed up about thirty foot and closed my eyes and just run till there wadn't nothin' under me."

Scott was soon followed by William Sloan, twenty-four, an African American from Louisville, Kentucky. Sloan, who was awaiting trial on auto theft charges, didn't know Scott at the time of the breakout, but did see the opportunity that was being presented to him and decided to make his escape. And like Scott, he had no trouble jumping off the second-story roof and running away. The third escapee, Roy Dill Collins, was acquainted with Scott, having been a partner with him in a previous escape a year earlier, which resulted in the kidnapping and rape of two women. The pair was not apprehended until they hit Louisiana. This flight from justice also resulted in a life sentence for Wilmer Scott.

Anyway, Collins, who must have decided there was a safer way of getting off the roof than just leaping into the air, sat down on the ledge, and, as gently as possible, dropped to the ground. However, jumping off the roof might have been the better way to go, for as soon as Collins hit the lawn, he felt his leg snap. Later, he may have come to believe that breaking his leg that afternoon was one of the best things that could have happened to him, given what Scott and Sloan would be involved in over the next ten or twelve hours. Still, Collins would receive an additional charge of attempted escape, producing a longer prison sentence.

"After reaching Collins," Evelyn Green testified, "I yelled to some people on the upper floors trying to get some help...Shortly afterward Steve Meilinger appeared in (the) window and I said 'Steve, send help. Your prisoners are getting out.' Before anyone got down to help us, the prisoners started throwing cigarettes out the window." Green then reached her hand into her purse, and the convicts, apparently believing she was reaching for a weapon, quickly backed away from the window. At almost the same time, an officer ran up to Collins, handcuffed him, and decided to stand guard over his prisoner. But Gail Chasteen, who didn't want the others getting away, pleaded with the officer to give chase, assuring him that she and Green would stay with Collins, who was now moaning loudly and obviously not going anywhere, but the officer refused to move.

Once on the ground, it took Scott and Sloan less than a minute to cross the street and enter the Sayre parking lot. Ewalt, being in the first car in line and whose doors were unlocked, was an easy target and immediately taken hostage by the pair. As Ewalt would later testify, "I was in the first car in line...

and (I) was parked to the right of the driveway. I had been sitting there approximately five or ten minutes when both doors were jerked open…Scott came in on the passenger's side door and Sloan pushed me out from under the driver's seat and jumped in. Scott then stated they were escaped prisoners with life sentences hanging over their heads. He went on to say he had a knife, and he would slit my throat if I made one move. I told them they were crazy, and I tried to get out of the car. I began to struggle and attempted to get the keys. Every time Sloan attempted to take off, I would put my foot on the break. I was also screaming and attempting to blow the horn as much as possible."

Although many people witnessed this, no one attempted to intervene. This both surprised and bothered Ewalt, who spoke of it later to a local news reporter from *the Lexington Herald-Leader*: "It was a few minutes before we finally got out of the parking lot because of the struggling and my pushing on the brake pedal. As the car pulled onto the alley way, it stalled and I again started screaming and blowing the horn" Sloan then reached down and yanked the shoe off the foot Ewalt was using to step on the brake, and threw it out the window. As Scott grabbed both of her legs to keep her still, Sloan punched her on the left side of the jaw. Scott then grabbed a magnetic flashlight from the dash and threatened to crush her skull if she didn't stop fighting them.

Once the car was out of the Sayre parking lot, Sloan made a number of turns as Scott gave directions. Every time a police car was seen in the distance,

Sloan would hit the brakes and change directions. Soon Ewalt became so confused, she didn't know where they were, and thought they might be driving in circles. "Finally we ended up on Sixth Street. Scott told Sloan we had to get out of here, and Scott asked me where I lived. I wouldn't tell him anything, and he stuck me again and cursed me. He said, 'You tell me where you live or we will kill you right here. You probably have kids at home, and we will take care of them after we find where you live.'" When she told them she had a boy and a girl at home, Scott threatened to rape the girl and "cut her up so I wouldn't know who she was."

By now, Scott was getting even more agitated because Ewalt still didn't recognize anything, but she did say if they could find Broadwa,y she could find her way home. Luckily, Sloan knew the way to Broadway, and shortly they were on New Circle Road heading away from town.

Obviously fearful of taking two crazed individuals into her home, Ewalt begged them to let her go. Of course, her request was denied, so she then pleaded with them not to hurt her children. Both men promised not to harm her kids, adding they were family men themselves; still, Scott continued to warn her, declaring at one point as they neared her house that he was going to kill her because of two parked police cars in two different driveways. Scott was so paranoid; he believed that Ewalt had somehow "set them up." But she quickly assured him this wasn't true; the police cars belonged to officers who lived in those houses and weren't looking for him.

As they pulled into her driveway at 1888 Charlbury Court, Scott again warned her he'd kill her if she made even one wrong move. With strained emotion, Ewalt told authorities, "When we got out of the car, the little girl next door, Arianna Jordan, came up to me and said, 'Hi.' She looked at the men and I told her to go home." But Arianna refused to move and Ewalt had to tell her several more times before the child returned home.

Once inside the house, Scott placed Ewalt in a chair in the kitchen, and while Sloan held a knife to her throat, he went throughout the house looking for the children. Moments later, Scott returned with Ewalt's eleven-year old son Paul, and while holding a knife to Paul's throat, walked him back into the kitchen, forcing him to sit in a chair near to his mother. Ewalt wasted no time instructing her son to be obedient and to do everything they asked of him. Scott again left the kitchen, only to return a minute later saying that a kid was outside and that Ewalt should "Call him in."

Opening the door, which leads out to the patio, she saw her "twelve- year-old daughter was out there cleaning her bike, and I called her to come in the house, and I got her in front of me, and we went back into the kitchen. And all three of us sat down, and I told Dena the same thing I had told Paul, 'Sit down and don't say or do anything and do exactly as you are told.'"

Only a moment before calling Dena inside, Scott reminded Ewalt what he'd do to her daughter if she tried anything. "He seemed very keyed up," Ewalt told police, "like something was going to pop in him…he kept going over the fact that he was going to rape my daughter." But Scott would not rape the girl. And perhaps because time was a factor - Mr. Ewalt was due home soon from work - Scott and Sloan made preparations to leave their hostages.

Scott then took Dena to Paul's room and bound her hands and feet with drapery cord. After laying her on the bed, he took one of Paul's baseball shirts and stuffed it into her mouth. Just as Scott was binding Mrs. Ewalt's hands with a cut telephone cord, a neighbor friend of Paul's began knocking on the kitchen door. Scott instructed Sloan to bring the boy inside the house, but Ewalt begged him not to, saying she could send him away. Sloan stood behind the door as Ewalt sent the boy home.

Soon, Scott and Sloan were back in the Ewalt car, heading north. With them they carried an old .22 rifle, without any ammunition; various knives; and money taken from Ewalt's purse. Fortunately, the Ewalts would survive their ordeal, but the psychological scars would last far into the future. Sadly, the next family would not be so lucky.

Eighteen-year-old Francine Barnes, a senior at Sayre and editor of the school newspaper, *The Sooth Sayre,* left school soon after Ewalt's abduction. It's not known whether she was aware of what had happened that afternoon, but it is known she arrived home alone, and her fourteen-year-old brother, Johnny, would be staying late at the school for football practice. Their father, the Reverend John K. Barnes, would pick Johnny up after practice and arrive home about dinnertime. Mrs. Mary Agnes Barnes, soon to be the only surviving member of the family, was in Louisville attending a conference of the Episcopal Church.

The Barnes' home, at Rt. 3 Russell Cave Road, was both picturesque and isolated. According to an article published in *The Lexington Herald-Leader*: "Though there are neighbors on horse farms within a quarter of a mile of the Barnes place, the trees are so situated that no other homes are visible from the Barnes home." Whatever fateful event led the two escapees to the Barnes' home remains a mystery, but it is believed by some in authority that Scott and Sloan may have watched Francine entering her home, and decided to take advantage of the situation. This much has been ascertained from later statements made by both men:

After parking the Ewalt's car in the rear of the Barnes' residence, they gained access to the house through an unlocked door. Upon entering, they found Francine standing there in a bathrobe. During the next few minutes, Scott took the girl around the house, locking all of the doors and windows. He also cut the wires to a home-to-car-communication system Mr. Barnes had installed some years earlier. He then searched the house for weapons, finding a shotgun, several rifles, and a pair of Smith & Wesson .38 revolvers. Scott kept both handguns and the shotgun, but stuffed the rifles behind the couch in the living room.

He then asked Francine when the rest of the family

would be coming home, and she said she expected her father and brother home at any time. When Reverend Barnes and his son finally did walk through the door, they found themselves at the mercy of the escapees. Scott, in a rambling statement later given to police said, "So I waited until they stepped through the door and cocked the pistol, and I told them that I was an escaped convict and that I was trying to get away, and I didn't want any trouble and I didn't want to hurt anyone and I made them sit down on the couch. Well, everything went along then alright for a couple of hours, and I told them when it got dark I was gonna take the car and leave."

Up until this night, Wilmer Elvis Scott had never killed anyone; that is, nothing in his long criminal record reflects that. According to his FBI rap sheet, Scott's crimes included: auto theft, assault and battery, armed robbery, fugitive (two counts) and rape. Today however, Scott would launch himself into that ultimate of all deeds — Murder!

At some point in their ordeal, the stress of the situation overcame the good judgment of the Reverend Barnes, and he began to shout at Scott. Of course, it didn't help matters that the two fugitives had been drinking the whiskey and wine found earlier in the Barnes home. In any event, Sloan said the tension built between the two men, with Barnes telling Scott he knew what kind of person he was. "That his soul was going to hell for what he had done and people like him belonged in the electric chair." Scott's own version is no less volatile. "He sat there a while and he started running his jaws and getting smart and I told him, 'I said Mister, I'm nervous, I'm tired… don't give me no trouble. Please, just shut your mouth.' 'Well (Barnes said) I'm a preacher and I'll tell you…' 'You ain't no preacher, (Scott responded) you ain't nothin'…I'm supposed to be the scum of the earth, I'm supposed to be sorry. Goddamn it, you got whiskey in every…icebox in this house, and beer in every icebox, wine! You got a house full of guns,…you are sitting there cussing like a sailor, and you tell me you are supposed to be a minister?"

In the midst of their shouting, Scott shot the reverend through the feet with the .410 shotgun. After this, everything was quiet for a while. Had it all ended here, Barnes would have recovered from his wounds. But the violence was only just beginning. According to Sloan, Barnes again started arguing with Scott and complained he was losing the circulation in his arms and hands, as they were tied behind his back. Upon hearing this, Scott loosened the restraints, but left Barnes in the chair still bound around the ankles. Sloan said it was while he was using the bathroom that he heard a shot and raced back into the room just in time to see Scott pushing Barnes back into the chair. Sloan could see the reverend had been shot, and that he did in fact appear dead. Scott told Sloan - and he would tell the police the same thing - that he shot Barnes with the pistol because he lunged at him.

Only minutes later, Scott took young Johnny Barnes, his hands still bound behind his back, and shot him once through the head with the .38 pistol. After this, Francine was taken to the bathroom where Scott fired a single bullet from the revolver into her head, killing

44

her instantly. He then ordered Sloan to drag the reverend's body into the bathroom, where Francine and Johnny had already been dumped.

When the bodies were recovered a little after 4 a.m., both Johnny and his father were dressed, but Francine was nude. Not surprisingly, she'd been raped, and when Scott was questioned about this, he at first said he didn't rape her, but then confessed he couldn't remember whether he raped her or not. Yet, when he was asked if Sloan raped the girl, his mind was crystal clear: "If that nigger had touched that white girl, I would have killed him," said Scott, quickly adding, "I was going to kill that nigger when we got to Ohio anyway."

He also said he believed Sloan knew he would kill him, and Sloan would do his best to get away from him. Later, he would comment on Sloan's role in the crime by saying: "I don't think Sloan – I didn't know him at the time we were in the Federal lockup. I don't think the man knew how much time I had. I don't think he realized how desperate I was, and I don't think he really realized the full extent of it until I got a gun in my hand. And I don't think he approved of what happened, but I don't think he was going to take a chance and start an argument with me, or mess with me in any way"

Sometime between 11:15 and 11:30 p.m., the two men took the keys to Reverend Barnes car and again headed north, this time on U.S. 27, and stayed on this road until they came to Fisher's motel in Falmouth Kentucky. Elva Harper had been the night clerk of the motel for the past three months, and according to an article published in *The Courier-Journal,* he had a foreboding, or a premonition, concerning his upcoming death, telling his landlord, Sam Shewalter, "You know, I might get killed out there."

After robbing the cash drawer, Harper was forced to open Room 5 where David Stidham, thirty-two, and twenty-seven-year-old Wendell McKenzie were sleeping. Within seconds, both men were shot and left for dead, yet both would survive. Sleeping next door in Room 6, were brothers David and Monroe Sizemore, of Thousandsticks, Kentucky. All four men had been working in the Falmouth area for several weeks and were planning to return home. But the Sizemore brothers would never return home – at least not alive. As Scott screamed at them to turn over their car keys, he started shooting and killed them both. Elva Harper's premonition came true as well: He was murdered as he tried to run out of the room.

Scott and Sloan then switched vehicles, this time stealing a car registered to the wife of Monroe Sizemore. The two continued driving north on U.S. 27, but a little before 2 a.m., they were noticed traveling at a high rate of speed by Sergeant Jack Westwood, of the Highland Heights Police Department, and a chase ensued. As Sergeant Westwood relayed the information to the dispatcher, he was informed of the Falmouth murders and their possible involvement in the crime. Westwood asked for backup, but before help could arrive, Scott and Sloan, though heavily armed and facing only one man, decided to surrender.

When Scott was later questioned about this and asked whether or not he intended to kill Westwood, he said yes, but Westwood refused to walk up to the car, and as such, "didn't play fair."

In just ten hours, six people had been murdered and two wounded. The emotional toll on those who survived the killing spree would last a lifetime. Later that morning, Scott and Sloan waived their right to remain silent and gave full confessions. Before getting started, however, Scott demanded coffee and something to eat, saying, "I ain't had nothin' to eat in twenty-four hours, and after I get my coffee I'll make any statement you want to hear." Once statements had been taken of the two, Scott and Sloan were transferred from Falmouth to the Kentucky State Police Post in Dry Ridge, Kentucky. Once again, both men were advised of their constitutional rights, but it was clear Scott had something else to say, not just about his crimes, but about his future. Sergeant Sparks later added the following to his report:

"During the trip, Scott, in Sloan's presence, stated to me that he felt bad that he'd killed six people and stated that he would never go to trial; that he would die before that, and if he did go to trial... all he could get was life, and he was already serving one life sentence. He stated that he would escape again, and he would kill a lot more people, but he didn't want that to happen." Scott said he wished the death penalty "was still in effect because he deserved it and was ready to die."

Scott soon made good on his promise. In early

February 1974, just three months after the murders, he set fire to his mattress in his cell at Eddyville State Penitentiary. Yet even with burns over one hundred percent of his body, he would not die for two days; this was the last of four suicide attempts while being housed at Eddyville.

William Sloan, however, would face an earthly judgment for his crimes, and would be convicted of the rape of Francine Barnes, robbery, kidnapping, and "aiding and abetting" Scott in his murderous rampage. All of this netted him numerous life sentences; all of them without the possibility of parole.

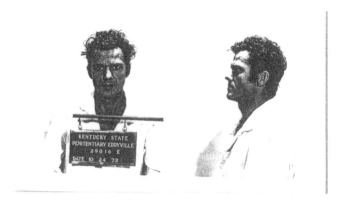

A pure homicidal psychopath, Wilmer Scott had no trouble killing defenseless people, but refused to shoot-it-out with a single police officer.

The Geraldine Ewalt residence

Located near the federal building, the Sayre School would be the starting point for Wilmer Scott and William Sloan's rampage

THE BOXHILL MURDERS

In June of 1977, Dennis Boehm, a Jefferson County Police officer assigned to Emergency Medical Services, responded to a call at 3200 Boxhill Lane, located just outside the Louisville city limits. Boxhill, commonly known to those accustomed to living under its gaze, is an elegant, thirty-two room Georgian Colonial Mansion sitting atop a bluff overlooking the Ohio River.It was an unlikely run for Officer Boehm to be making, given this genteel area east of Louisville, filled with old homes and even older money, but the police dispatcher had radioed that a man there had gone, "berserk (and that) shots had been fired."

When Boehm and his team arrived, they entered the house through an open front door and followed a hallway that took them into the kitchen. Here they found smashed eggshells on the countertops and floor. And like the front door, the back door was standing wide open, too. Within ten minutes of being in the house, the telephone rang and a women who identified herself as "the aunt," warned those in the house to watch out for the son, who might have a gun and may even attempt to kill them. But the house was now empty, and the danger, at least temporarily, had passed, for the "son," twenty-eight-year-old Kirk Ellington Tiff, was, even before police arrived, on his way to the hospital where he would be mentally evaluated.

Tiff, the only child of Shirley Alexander from a previous marriage, had not lived with his mother and stepfather since his teenage years, at which time he became unmanageable, and decided to live with his father, Donald Tiff, in Colorado. But living with his father would not prove to be a panacea either, and by the late 1960s, Kirk, like so many other young people at the time, immersed himself in the drug culture. And this, perhaps, was the beginning of his deep decent into mental illness - an illness that would first drive him into fits of rage, and eventually to murder.

It is unknown whether Kirk was admitted to the hospital that June or merely treated and released. What is known, however, is that before the month was out, Kirk, again, was going off the deep end, and it was at this time that Shirley Alexander telephoned John Hicks, a long-time friend of the family, who was also their attorney. The following year, he testified concerning his meeting with the Alexanders and Kirk Ellington Tiff:

"I went up, I guess it was about 2:00 p.m....and (I) sat there and talked with them and with him for several hours. I couldn't make any sense with him. And she and I went into an adjoining room, and I suggested that she go down to the hospital and see if she could take out a warrant for him. So she went and did this. Bob and I were still there talking with him, and he was talking about going to Mexico or Canada or Nashville."

When Kirk decided his destination should be California, John Hicks and Mr. Alexander wasted no time getting him to the airport and putting him on a plane. And soon the jet carrying Kirk lifted off the runway and headed into the western sky, and with it, came a great sense of relief to the Alexanders. But that sense of relief would be short lived, as the nightmare would begin all over again in the fall.

It is important to note here that the Alexanders were very private people. Mr. Alexander, while always courteous and polite with everyone he encountered, was not an overly sociable person. As such, he would never permit himself to talk openly about Kirk with just anyone, no matter how terrible the situation might be. Shirley Alexander, on the other hand, was quite forthright with her friends and others concerning the dangers they were facing. Indeed, she felt her son was capable of murdering her, her husband, even her little dog. And it appears, at least from the subsequent testimony of friends and neighbors, if anything was to be done about Kirk, she would have to take the necessary legal steps.

When Kirk returned to Boxhill on October 14, 1977, Shirley Alexander wrote the following brief note on her kitchen calendar:

"Kirk arrived this a.m."

As their attorney, John Hicks remembered the event: "She told me that he was back and was causing them a lot of trouble. He would stay up most of the night and rant and rave, and she was really scared of him, and I think Bob was too." Hicks again suggested that she should obtain a mental inquest warrant, but she hesitated this time, fearing what Kirk would do once he was released. Hicks then suggested she send him to his office where the two could talk privately. In late November, Kirk Tiff did sit down with John Hicks for a final conversation, but again, it would do nothing to alter the course of events. Kirk was beyond help and Hicks knew it, but if Shirley would not take out the warrant, he would do all he could to defuse this volatile situation:

"He thought he was a musician," Hicks testified. "He played a guitar (and) I talked to him, and tried to encourage him to get a job, go somewhere where he could play his music…and get away from them, and again, I wasn't able to get through to him."

At 7:00 p.m., on November 28, Mrs. Ella Hilliker received a call from Shirley Alexander, and while their conversation did not immediately include Kirk, Ella could feel the apprehension in her voice and knew something was terribly wrong. When asked about it, Shirley replied, "Oh, it's Kirk, he's just been threatening me." Of course, it was now beyond mere threats, as Shirley would soon confess, telling

Ella Hilliker that Kirk "had lunged at her and was frothing at the mouth."

Perhaps for the first time, Mrs. Alexander truly believed her son had completely lost his mind. Even so, there would be no warrant issued, and the Alexander's fate was now completely sealed. Before saying goodbye to each other, Ella asked her friend if she wanted to come over to her home for the evening, an invitation Shirley politely declined. Still, Ella Hilliker quickly added that should she change her mind, she could always come over later. With this, the two women said goodbye.

Another close friend of Shirley Alexander was Mrs. Wanda Moore. Like Ella Hilliker, Moore knew all about Kirk's violent tendencies and, as Shirley had recently explained to her, that Kirk "had just blown his mind with drugs." Moore would also tell authorities that Shirley "was terribly afraid. And she came to my house often, you know, as I could get away, or she could get away, and we were together as much as we could be." The last time the two had spoken to each other was by telephone, probably on Monday, December 5, when they made plans to have lunch together the following Friday.

During that week, the Alexanders, who had purchased a new home, were going to be very busy packing up boxes and getting the new house ready to move into. "I had talked to her on Monday, or Tuesday," Wanda Moore remembered, "of that week, and she said 'I'm busy packing, so I won't be talking to you until I see you Friday.' So I didn't bother calling. I had to keep my grandchild that weekend and all the following week because he had pneumonia, so I couldn't go out, but I kept calling. So on Tuesday I said 'well, I'm not going to wait any longer.'" At this time, Mrs. Moore stopped trying to call her friend and contacted the police.

Responding to the call was Officer Edward Brodt, of the Jefferson County Police. After obtaining the necessary information for the missing persons report, Officer Brodt left the Moore residence and drove the short distance to 3200 Boxhill Lane. Upon arrival, he found the main gate locked. However, a side entrance through the gate had been left standing partially open, and from here it was just a short walk to the house. There wasn't a sign of life anywhere, and a knock on the front door produced only the sound of a barking dog.

As Brodt made his way around to the rear of the house he peered into various windows, but there was still no sign of Mr. or Mrs. Alexander. And then Brodt noticed "a rear screen door unlocked, with the interior door partially open. Upon entering, it appeared the house was not occupied, and I detected a foul odor. As I approached the hallway, I observed a male Caucasian lying (on) the kitchen floor obviously deceased...as I proceeded through the house, I found another body...a white female lying in the entrance way of the kitchen. I also observed two butcher knives, one on the kitchen cabinet by the white male, the other on the kitchen floor by the female."

Kirk Ellington Tiff had made good on his threats.

Robert Alexander was found lying face down in a large pool of blood. He had been stabbed fifteen times and had suffered a severe head wound, defined by authorities as blunt trauma. Nearby the body lay a fireplace poker with a broken handle. Shirley Alexander was found lying face down in the doorway, which adjoins the sunroom and the kitchen. But she had not been killed here, as virtually no blood surrounded the body. However, several feet away were two large pools of blood on the kitchen floor, and a significant blood-spatter pattern on the cabinets and the surrounding area.

Just why Kirk felt the need to drag his mother into the doorway leading to the sunroom, is unknown. Underneath the body was a small, crumpled up floor rug, heavily stained with blood, that originally lay at the spot where Shirley was killed. Officer Brodt radioed his supervisor with the news that his missing persons "call" had now turned into a double homicide. And as other units began responding, his search of the house continued.

When lead Detective, Don Hillebrandt, and Detective Robert Smith arrived, Brodt led them into the kitchen to view the bodies. Still guarding the decaying remains was Shirley Alexander's white terrier dog. Evidently, the dog had not only been lying in the blood, but drinking it, as evidenced by the smears around its mouth, face, and chest. When detectives tried to approach the bodies, the dog began barking wildly and jumping around, making it difficult for them to do their job. After driving the dog away into a small room adjacent to the kitchen, a patrol officer contacted the Humane Society to have the animal removed from the home and not to destroy it.

Shortly after the arrival of Smith and Hillebrandt, other homicide detectives began pouring into the house, as did police photographers, the fingerprint crew, and other evidence teams. Yet, from the moment police first discovered the murdered bodies of this east Louisville couple, Kirk became the main suspect in the case. Over the next several days, authorities would hear from those who were aware of the threats Kirk had made against his mother and stepfather, and how fearful Shirley Alexander had become. And other evidence, soon to be discovered in the house, and in Colorado, would provide detectives with a vivid picture of the killer's activities during and after the murders.

Later that evening, Chaplain Fleenor of the Jefferson County Police, drove over to Wanda Moore's house and broke the sad news that her friend had been killed. While the chaplain and Mrs. Moore were talking, Detective Hillebrandt telephoned to ask if she knew the name of Kirk's father, which she did not, only that he lived in Colorado. However, after hanging up with the detective, Moore called Donald and Ella Hilliker and told them the terrible news. In turn, the Hillikers telephoned the detectives at Boxhill and offered to help the investigators in any way possible, adding that Kirk's father still lived in Colorado and that his name is Donald Tiff.

Meanwhile, Detective Bobby Shanks, who was assisting with the interviewing of the neighbors, discovered that Mrs. Alexander's beige, 1971 Mercury station wagon was missing. The vehicle, still bearing Illinois plates from their recent move from Chicago, had evidently not been seen for at least several days. In all likelihood, police believed, Kirk Tiff was either already in Colorado or well on his way.

At 9:45 a.m., on December 14, Hillebrandt telephoned Detective John L. Weber of the Denver Colorado Homicide Bureau, to inform him of the double homicide in Kentucky, and that the suspect, Kirk Ellington Tiff, might be in the area attempting to contact his father. Hillebrandt also gave him information concerning Shirley Alexander's station wagon, as well as Donald Tiff's current address.

By 11 a.m., a Denver Police officer had located the Mercury station wagon parked at the corner of Severn Place and Olive Street. Neighbors said the car had been parked there for about a week. Lying on the front seat were the ignition key and a bloody glove.

Having located the station wagon, Denver Police set up a command post one block away for surveillance, and by twelve o'clock, they were ready to enter Donald Tiff's house on Pontiac Avenue. Yet, before the word to go was given, Mr. Tiff was observed driving up to his house and was immediately stopped and escorted into the command post where the situation was explained to him.

Donald Tiff quickly acknowledged that he'd heard about the murders in Kentucky, apparently earlier in the morning through a local news broadcast. He also told police that Kirk had come to his home on the evening of December 8, and had "numerous lacerations on his hands." These lacerations would come as no surprise to detectives in Louisville, for the killer of the Alexanders had left his own blood trail throughout the house, and in several of the bathroom sinks, blood soaked towels and bandages had been found. As soon as Donald Tiff saw how badly his son's hands were damaged, he immediately drove him to the emergency room of Colorado General Hospital. Tiff assured police that he hadn't seen Kirk since that night, but he did mention that his son might seek out a friend of his living in Aurora, Colorado. But as police would soon discover, Tiff would not be found in Aurora.

By early afternoon, warrant number 160669-14 had been issued in Kentucky, charging Kirk Ellington Tiff with two counts of first degree murder, and one count of unlawful taking of a vehicle. Evidently, the hunt for Tiff was extensive indeed. Hundreds of uniformed officers were keeping their eyes open, as were dozens of detectives. Still, Kirk was nowhere to be found, and as the hours rolled by, it appeared a deranged killer was either doing an excellent job of hiding himself or had fled Denver altogether.

Yet Tiff's ability to elude police was not due to his own powers, but a simple human error on the part of authorities, who mistakenly believed he'd been treated at Colorado General and released. And they would not learn of their mistake until the morning of the following day.

On the bitterly cold morning of December 15, 1977, Detective Weber stopped by Colorado General Hospital to view Tiff's medical record of December 8. In what must have come as a shock to this veteran law officer, the receptionist informed him that Kirk Tiff had been admitted to the hospital on December 8, and was in fact still being treated as an in-patient by Doctor R. Murphy for "extensive cuts to the hands." Upon hearing this, Weber asked Doctor Murphy, as well as the head of hospital security, to accompany him to Tiff's room, where he was placed under arrest and read his constitutional rights.

Back in Louisville, authorities were building an air-tight case against the killer, and were, ever so slowly, gaining a better picture of the events leading up to the murders and when the Alexanders were most likely killed. Within days of the story hitting the Louisville newspapers, police received a call from twenty-six-year-old David Dumeyer, an employee of Roppels Market, who'd known Shirley Alexander for about five years. Dumeyer said that on December 7, while driving along Shelbyville Road, he noticed a beige Mercury station wagon with wood paneling on the side and was certain it belonged to Mrs. Alexander. And a quick look at the license plate confirmed his suspicions. As Dumeyer pulled alongside the wagon, he saw the driver was a "white male with blondish hair, kind of long ...he kept looking straight ahead and his eyes appeared to be bloodshot and looked like he was crying." Dumeyer watched him as he entered an expressway ramp, no doubt the beginning of his journey west to Colorado.

Later, Detective Hillebrandt would show Dumeyer the photographs of five white males, whose names and personal information had been blocked out. With little more than a glance, Dumeyer pointed to the mug shot of Tiff, identifying him as the driver of Shirley Alexander's station wagon. Because Dumeyer saw him on the afternoon of the seventh, authorities believe the Alexanders were killed late on the sixth or in the early morning hours of the seventh.

As Tiff sat in the homicide office of the Denver Police Department, he remained silent. Having fled across state lines, authorities in both states were aware he might fight extradition back to Kentucky, but he could be successful for only so long. This is exactly what happened, and so, as the legal paper work began to churn, the Jefferson County Police continued their investigation.

On March 1, 1978, an inquisition was held in Louisville to determine the cause of death for Robert and Shirley Alexander. Testifying were police officers, friends of the Alexanders, and their attorney John Hicks. From this testimony emerged a picture - albeit a partial one - of the fear and apprehension that had been tearing at the couple in the weeks prior to their deaths. Wanda Moore stated she had seen Robert Alexander only days before the murders as he was coming out the front gate of his home, but he did not speak to her. Just why the Alexander's refused to do anything about Kirk before it was too late is unknown. However, when Hillebrandt questioned Hicks about this, he responded that Shirley Alexander was "a very religious person and a good mother, and didn't want to do anything to hurt Kirk." Perhaps she really believed Kirk didn't want to hurt her either, and that somehow, his screaming fits and frothing at the mouth would simply go away, much like a bad dream. But this was not a bad dream, and soon Kirk would explode into a homicidal rage, and the fate of the Alexanders would be sealed. And Kirk, with a fireplace poker in one hand and a butcher knife in the other, would quickly overwhelm and kill his mother and stepfather, probably in a matter of minutes.

As the inquisition came to its expected end, the cause of death was determined to be: "Shirley Pierce Alexander met her death on approx. December 6, 1977 (found December 13, 1977) and it was due to exsanguinations, multiple stab wounds, and from the evidence we have heard, we believe it was: murder, at the hand of Kirk Ellington Tiff." The report continued, "Robert E. Alexander met his death on approx. December 6,1977, (found December 13, 1977) and it was due to : Internal Hemorrhage, multiple stab wounds, and from the evidence we have heard, we believe it was: murder, at the hand of Kirk Ellington Tiff."

In June of 1978, Tiff would give up his fight against extradition and willingly return to Kentucky. Even so, Kirk Tiff would never stand trial for the murders, having been diagnosed a paranoid schizophrenic by the medical experts, and as such, unable to assist in his own defense. Of course, such a diagnosis could change, and so, over the next nine years, state prosecutors would charge Tiff anew with the crime on four different occasions, yet each time he would be declared unfit to stand trial.

Finally, in November 1986, a Jefferson County circuit judge forever dismissed all charges against Tiff, declaring: "he had been denied his constitutional rights to due process and a speedy trial." Of course, this now meant that Mr. Tiff could be released back into society someday, if the doctors evaluating him decided it was safe to do so. One month later, however, all of this would change, as Tiff would pass sentence upon himself. Early one morning in late December, he would be found unconscious on the bathroom floor at Louisville's Central State Hospital, an electrical-cord wrapped around his neck and attached to a handrail in the shower stall. For four days he remained on life-supports. During this period, four brain scans were administered, and each time results were the same: Kirk Tiff was already dead, at least, in a neurological sense. And so, at 4:50 p.m., on December 22, 1986, the plug was pulled, and twelve minutes later, Kirk Ellington Tiff was declared legally dead.

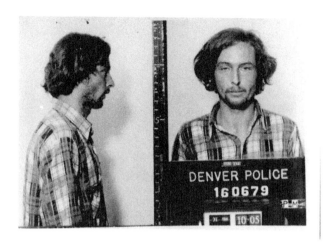

Kirk Tiff, after his arrest in Denver

The beautiful estate known as Boxhill was an unlikely place for carnage

JEALOUSY IS FOREVER

At 8:45 p.m. on the cold night of December 6, 1993, Mary F. Byron left her job early at the JCPenney hair salon located at the Mall St. Matthews in St. Matthews, Kentucky, a city that is a part of metropolitan Louisville, Kentucky. It was Mary's twenty-first birthday, and she was planning to meet her friend Jana at her house around 9 p.m. when the two young women would then go out for a few drinks.

Mary had already celebrated her birthday with her family and friends the day before, so tonight she would unwind with a friend and concentrate on a future that was beginning to look bright once again after a period of darkness. For on this night, Mary would not only be celebrating her twenty-first birthday, that last proverbial leap into adulthood, but she would be rejoicing in her new-found freedom after severing a relationship she found stifling, and worst of all, was making her afraid for her life.

Abiding by employee rules, Mary had parked her car

with the other workers at the far end of the parking lot, allowing the hordes of Christmas shoppers plenty of room to fight over the good spaces closer to the mall's entrance. Situated directly across from where Mary was parked was a wooded area, and beyond that, an apartment complex, and a rather large stream, known as Beargrass Creek, cut a path through the woods at this point.

Unknown to Mary, someone was hiding in those thick, dark woods, watching her as she walked to her car, waiting for just the right moment to emerge from the darkness, pistol in hand. As Mary waited for her car to warm up, she probably watched as two other workers from the salon drove out of the lot, but no one will ever know whether she caught a glimpse of the figure running up to her car. What is certain, however, is that, within a minute of Mary entering her car, eight rapidly fired shots from a 9 mm handgun discharged at point-blank range just outside of her driver's side window sent Mary Byron slumping into the passenger seat. She had been hit seven times and died almost instantly. Within hours police would be looking for her ex-boyfriend, twenty-three-year-old Donovan Dale Harris.

Donovan Harris and Mary Byron had been dating for about four years, and while their relationship was sometimes on or off, Harris became quite a fixture in the Byron home. Mary's parents, John and Patricia, had treated Harris like he was a part of their family, loaning him their car when his vehicle was in the shop, and letting him borrow a television set when his wasn't working. At Mrs. Byron's insistence, they told Donavan he could do his laundry at their house and, as such, save him a little money. The Byrons were very loving and freely made Donavan Harris a part of their family.

Andrea Ulmer, who'd been best friends with Mary from kindergarten until the time of the murder, often had long talks with her friend, and according to Andrea, the first two years Mary and Donovan dated, everything appeared normal. But in the last couple of years, Harris became extremely jealous and possessive, telling Mary he didn't want her going to parties unless he, too, could go along. He would also demand she look straight ahead while they were in the car, as he didn't want her looking out her window at any other men. Mary also confided to Andrea that even if a male friend merely spoke to her, Harris would begin spewing out threats. At first she did as Harris asked, but such control could not last forever, and as Mary began to resist, arguments between the couple increased. Indeed, Byron confessed to a co-worker at the salon that her 1993 trip to Florida with Harris consisted mostly of arguments. In August of that year, Mary ended her relationship with Donovan.

Evidently, the breakup drove Harris into an emotional spiral that sometimes produced crying and his begging her to come back to him. At other times, there would be threats of violence. Ulmer told police, "Donovan would repeat these things over and over again." Mary also told Andrea he threatened to kill her three cats if she didn't listen to him and give him another chance. As time went by, Harris began telling her he was going to kill himself – perhaps on his birthday – if she didn't come back, but this did not bring the desired results either.

Perhaps growing more and more frustrated, and knowing that Harris was unstable, perhaps dangerously unstable, Mary experienced a very real fear she could become one-half of a murder/suicide, and maybe in the very near future. However, the October 20 birthday of Harris passed without incident. Even so, Mary kept watching for any signs he might be stalking her, and she told her male friends to be on the lookout, too.

On Wednesday, November 17, 1993, Harris telephoned Mary saying he wanted to return the television her parents had loaned him. Mary, who did in fact want the television back, said she'd call him later and arrange a time for him to come over. But Harris wasn't about to wait for her call. The next day was Thursday, and like every Thursday, he knew it was Mary's regular day off from work. At approximately 9:40 a.m., the following morning, Donovan Harris arrived at the Byron home, television in hand. Mary allowed him to come inside. For a time, they stood in the living room talking. Harris again asking if the two of them could get back together. Yet the more Harris talked, the more unsettled Mary became, and with good reason, "Because he was saying things such as 'would you do anything for me if I had a pistol?'"

He then asked her if she would have sex with him one more time, promising to leave afterward. Harris also taunted her, asking her what she thought it would be like to be shot. When Mary answered she didn't know, Harris replied, he'd "heard it burns a little, but it doesn't hurt that much." Hearing this, Mary asked if he had a gun, but Harris said no. Then, perhaps for effect, he repeated the same taunting question.

Mary then turned the proverbial tables on Donovan, asking if he knew what it would feel like to be stabbed. As Harris answered that he didn't know, Mary grabbed a steak knife and pointed it at him. Unmoved by her threat, he quickly demanded she put the knife back in the rack. When Mary refused, he warned her again. This time she obeyed.

"What would be worse," Harris asked, "having sex with me, or dying?" Mary could stand it no longer. Although escape was hopeless, she started running toward her bedroom where she hoped to lock herself inside and telephone police. But Harris, who at that point pulled out a pistol from his pocket, quickly chased her down, finally gaining control of her at the top of the stairs leading to the basement. Here a struggle ensued, causing both of them to fall down the steps; Harris cut his hand on the way down. They remained on the basement floor for some time, just talking, and knowing she was at his mercy, Mary now changed tactics. She told Harris they could try again, that she had been unfair with breaking up and that she had just wanted time to think things through. But Harris did not believe her. Both of them were now crying (but for different reasons) and Mary had her face buried against the wall.

After attempting to kiss her, Donavan slipped off her

shoes and removed her jeans. This so enraged Mary that she slapped him, and Harris responded by hitting her back. Mary knew she didn't have the power to stop him from raping her; not only was he physically stronger but he had a handgun, and she believed he'd use it. "You know this is rape," she said, whereupon Harris dragged her to an exercise mat, pulled her pants down to her knees, and raped her, all the while holding her sweatshirt over her face because she was crying.

Within minutes of the rape, Harris admitted he'd made a mistake, saying he believed she would now call police. But Mary said no, for she was too ashamed to admit what had happened to her. She then asked if he was going to hurt her. Harris said no, but then ordered her upstairs. If Mary believed Harris was now going to leave she was greatly mistaken, as he insisted they sit on the couch awhile and talk. The distraught young woman would later tell police, that as Harris sat on the sofa he kept his hand in a duffel bag the entire time. When she asked him if he had another gun inside the bag, he told her not to worry about it.

Later that day, when Harris was arrested for the rape, he admitted they did indeed have sex, but it was consensual. However, a physical examination conducted by the University of Louisville Hospital only hours after the attack, revealed a small vaginal tear consistent with being raped. And now that Harris had been arrested, perhaps Mary could finally live a life free of the worry of what he might do to her.

But on December 6, all of Mary Byron's worries ended forever.

John King, a part-time security guard for Mall St. Matthews, had been patrolling the lot in his vehicle when he heard what he thought were three gunshots piercing the cold night air. As he looked in the direction from which he believed the firing had come, he could see "what looked like a cloud of smoke come up from the back of the parking lot." King immediately radioed mall security stating there might be a problem and he was going to investigate it. He also instructed them to call the St. Matthews Police Department and advise them of a possible shooting.

As King drove to the rear of the parking lot, he saw a figure fleeing into the woods. Seeing this, King shot past the employee cars, crossed the two-lane road that circles the mall, and shined his headlights out toward the woods in front of him. Unfortunately, whomever he saw running away had now disappeared into the trees.

Turning his vehicle around, King saw a car with both the passenger and driver's side windows shattered. Although he couldn't see anyone inside the car he could hear the engine racing. He also noticed a small hole punched through the metal in the lower portion of the passenger's side door. Being unarmed and alone, King kept looking all around as he approached Mary's car. From the moment he first heard the shots until now had been less than two minutes, so there wasn't a lot of time to think about what he was now seeing. Still, by the time he came close to the damaged car, he must have known this was more than a case of mere vandalism. His suspicions were quickly confirmed. As the mall security officer peered through the shattered car window, he saw the still form of a young woman slumped over the passenger seat, eyes open but sightless. Visible were three bullet holes in her neck, and it appeared to King the woman was already dead.

Running back to his car, he grabbed his radio and contacted the St. Matthews Police to confirm that a shooting had occurred at the mall. He then radioed mall security, asking specifically for Tim Close, who'd recently completed Emergency Medical Training. But even as he was speaking, King saw Close running toward him through the parking lot. While King kept looking out for trouble, Close checked the young woman for a pulse but found none. He then reached inside her car and switched the engine off.

At about this same time, the first police officer arrived, followed by a second patrolman thirty seconds later. Soon, dozens of officers, detectives, and a K-9 unit would arrive, as did Emergency Medical Services. And like Tim Close had done only moments before, paramedics felt for a pulse but did not find one. Leaving nothing to chance, they removed Mary's jacket, opened her shirt and attached a heart monitor, which confirmed the young woman was dead.

On this night, Mary's parents, along with Mary's friend, Jana, were decorating the artificial Christmas tree the Byrons had recently purchased. It must have been an especially good night for them, for not only was Mary starting to reclaim her life, but the source of the problem, Donovan Harris, was safely tucked away in jail. Or so they believed.

But when 9:00 p.m. turned into 9:15, and there was still no sign of their daughter, Patricia Byron asked her husband to drive the route Mary always used when coming home, just in case she was having car trouble. As John Byron was going out the door, his wife handed him her cellular phone. Mr. Byron had been gone only a short time when Andrea Ulmer called the house and asked Pat if Mary was home. She said no, and then Andrea asked if she and Jana had already left for their night out, and again the answer was no. When Andrea heard this she got a bad feeling, for she had just seen a news report on television saying a woman had been shot and killed at the mall, and she sensed it might be Mary. But when she mentioned this to Pat, the mother disregarded it, saying that Mary was fine and should be home anytime. After saying good bye to Andrea, Pat and Jana continued decorating the Christmas tree.

Although Mary had indeed had trouble with cars in the past, it was unlikely she was having trouble with her new 1993 Chevy Cavalier, so it probably came as no surprise to her dad she was not stranded along the roadway. But when he reached the mall, amidst the throngs of police and blue flashing lights, he would learn the awful truth of why Mary was not and would not come home again. Not long after this, Pat Byron was met with the terrible news from her parish priest,

Father Frank Imer. As Father Imer pulled into their driveway, Pat must have sensed something horrible was coming as she at first refused to open the door to let him come inside. Perhaps she believed opening the door meant she would be forced to hear something so awful she just couldn't face it.

Meanwhile, police had closed off the area around the mall and were searching the woods and the Mallgate Apartments, located on nearby Sherburn Lane. Several of Mary's co-workers watched and were horrified by something they noticed: "(They) started to get upset," one witness remembered, "when they realized it was their friend's vehicle and said she is dead because they are not doing anything for her."

Mary Byron died almost instantly, and according to the postmortem examination report: "the victim had been shot seven times on the left upper side of the body. There were entrance wounds on the left side of the breast and a wound about two inches above that wound. There was an entrance wound in the left upper arm and left upper shoulder. In the neck area there appears to be an entrance in the left neck, left chin, and one to the back of the neck about three inches down and to the rear of the ear. The three wounds in the neck appear to be the last wounds in the body due to the closeness of the entrance wounds. There appears to be four exit wounds, one being in the right upper shoulder, one just to the rear of the right ear, and two in the right panatela bone in the skull."

As police swarmed over the area around Mall St.

Matthews, Officer Robert J. Moster received some unexpected help: "A Captain Blakely from the McMahan Fire Department flagged me down around Sherburn Lane and Quails Run Road to let me know he had just seen a subject walking south on Mallgate property, and when the Jefferson County police helicopter flew over him, he ducked in between two apartments that face Sherburn Lane." Blakely described the individual as a white male wearing dark clothing.

Shortly after the murder, Harris telephoned his friend, Vincent Sullivan, who was working that evening at the B P station along Bardstown Road. Answering the phone that evening was assistant manager Dale Stewart, who later told police Harris forcefully asked to speak with Sullivan, as if he was demanding to talk with him. According to Stewart, she told Sullivan to take the call in the back office, and as she continued to listen in on their conversation, Harris allegedly blurted out: "I killed her, and now I'm going to kill myself." Upon hearing this, Stewart said, Sullivan started crying and became incoherent.

Vincent Sullivan's version, however, is quite different. According to Sullivan, Harris never mentioned Mary, but did say certain things that led him to believe that Harris might attempt to take his own life, and as a friend, Sullivan told authorities, he wanted to stop this from happening. Nevertheless, Sullivan and Stewart both agree they made at least two, if not three calls to the Jefferson County Police concerning the Harris call. When police learned that Harris had been released from jail, and his accuser, Mary Byron, had just been murdered, their investigation narrowed dramatically.

According to the investigative reports, about 9 p.m., Emily Hoffman was visiting her mother at 35 Summerfield Circle, in the Four Seasons Apartment complex: "My cousin and I were in the parking lot for about 15 minutes," Hoffman remembered, "and during that time, a man went into the fenced area where the dumpsters were located and threw something away...I personally did not pay any attention to the man, but my cousin said later that he caught her attention because he ran, or hurried over to the dumpster as soon as he got out of his car."

By 11:30 p.m., S.W.A.T. members of the Jefferson County Police were taking up positions around Harris's building. Over the next several hours, while the proper warrants were being obtained, numerous attempts were made to contact Harris by telephone and by loudspeaker. Officers were also listening from the hallway, outside of Harris's apartment, for any sound of the suspect, and S.W.A. T. team members, who'd already cleared the apartments adjoining Harris's, were listening for movement as well. But all was silent, and Harris either would not or could not respond. "Elements of the entry and response teams were pulled off to a similar designed apartment down the hall." stated the official S.W.A.T. report, "These officers conducted several walk throughs (sic) going over tactics to be used if a slow search is required."

With still no activity emanating from the suspect's dwelling, the police had little alternative but to enter the apartment. After opening the front door of Apartment Number 10, police waited several minutes before moving inside.

"After several minutes a distraction device was dispensed into the living room." The report continues, "A small fire was started on the floor...setting off the fire alarm. Coughs were heard coming from the apartment." Again, police called out to Harris, who still refused to answer. Tear gas was then fired into the back bedroom, but this also failed to rouse him. Yet again, a distraction device – better known as a flash-bang – was tossed into the room, setting off more fire alarms, but once more, Donovan Harris remained silent.

By now, it was clear to the S.W.A.T. team that a room by room search would have to be conducted, greatly increasing the danger for both the police and Harris. After securing the living room and the kitchen, the heavily armed men pressed onward: "With weapons covering down the hallway, flash-bangs were thrown into the doorway of both the bedroom and the bathroom. At this point, a third distraction device was introduced into the bedroom from down the hall. After the distraction device activated, the suspect could be heard in the bedroom. Several challenges were made with no response."

Once the team had reached the bedroom door, the report states that an Officer Conner: "mirrored the bedroom and bathroom (and) at this time a distraction device was placed in the bedroom. Lt. Milburn rolled out...positioning himself on the right side of the door…and began challenging the suspect to put his hands up." But apparently, Harris had no intention of obeying their commands: "The suspect was sitting in bed and a fire was burning with flames rising several feet into the air. Several challenges were given to the suspect who continued to place his hands under the cover of the bed, and then revealing them." But instead of killing Harris, who could have been reaching under the covers for a weapon, Lieutenant Milburn charged into the room and dived over the flames tackling Harris, who continued fighting as the two fell to the floor. Indeed, Harris kept fighting until several officers had him pinned, handcuffed, and carried out to the ambulance. Between his short siege, and his struggle with police, their suspect had sustained numerous injuries, including a burn on his ankle from one of the flash-bangs, which required several days of hospitalization.

And it would be during this time of recuperation at University of Louisville Hospital, that Harris would admit to Officer Larry Ethington that he killed Mary Byron. Later, police would discover he'd purchased the handgun used to kill her, on December 5, the day before the murder. Of course, in 1993, there wasn't a system set up like there is today, where a buyer must undergo an instant background check. And those who sold the pistol to Harris said he appeared perfectly normal, was polite, and looked rather like someone who had just come from church.

In August of 1995, Donovan Dale Harris was convicted of the November 18, 1993, rape, and the December 6, 1993, murder of Mary F. Byron. For the rape, he received a sentence of eighteen years. For the murder, he received a life sentence with the possibility of parole after twenty-five years. As of this writing (2015) Harris is still behind bars.

In March of 1994, Harris wrote a letter to Andrea Ulmer in which he asked her how she was doing, and most importantly, could she tell him, "anything & everything" about Mary, being that she was Mary's "closest friend." Harris ended his odd letter with one last request:

"When you visit Mary, give her a flower and tell her I love her… she was everything to me."

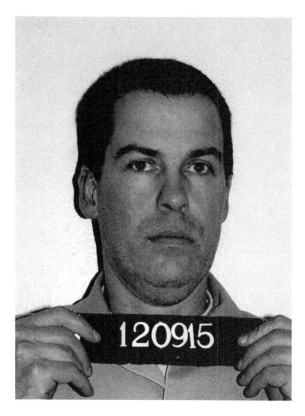

Feeling jilted, Donovan Harris decided to kill his girlfriend, Mary Byron, on her 21st birthday

THE ICE MAN

"In the early evening of December 5, 1978, Sheila Knox and her seven-year-old daughter, Donna, returned to their mobile home situated near Bowen, Powell County, Kentucky. Immediately upon entering, Mrs. Knox became apprehensive that something was wrong and turned to leave the trailer. Her exit was halted by a blow and resulting sharp pain in her shoulder that propelled her from the trailer.

As Sheila Knox was falling to the ground, she let out a loud, piercing scream. Fifteen-year-old Todd Ice, a church-going boy with an IQ of 136, wasted no time getting his two captives inside the trailer. Locking the door behind them, he instructed Donna and her mother to sit on the sofa while he closed the drapes. As Ice stood before them, he wondered out loud whether anyone had heard Sheila's scream.

Todd Ice was no stranger to the Knox family. Over the last several years, their mobile home had been burglarized on numerous occasions, and Ice, whose family had lived nearby for the last six years, was their only suspect. Later, friends of Ice would come forward and testify that Todd had acknowledged his involvement in the thefts, and apparently, December 5, 1978, was to be just another such incident. Just why Todd Ice chose this particular day to invade the Knox home remains a mystery. It's certain he was aware that Sylvester Knox was at work and would not return home for hours. But, it must also be assumed, that Ice realized Sheila and Donna Knox would soon be returning home on such a dark, cold, and rainy evening. And so, the true intentions of why Ice was in the Knox trailer that night is open to question. What is not in question, however, is what happened once Sheila and Donna arrived home.

Ice took mother and daughter into Donna's room and had them sit on the bed. Several minutes later, Ice gave Sheila a pillow and told her to lie down, but she kept insisting "she wasn't hurt that bad" adding that Todd should go home. Yet Todd made it clear he wasn't about to return home: "I'm going to wait till my mommy comes home." Sheila, however, kept telling Ice he should leave, so after a few minutes of this captive-captor exchange, he blurted out: "Hush, you're making me nervous, let me think." Ice then took a bed sheet and tied Sheila's hands and neck to the bedpost and bound her feet. During this time, Ice allowed Donna to hold the knife he had used to stab her mother only a short time earlier. When Ice picked up a piece of a metal pipe he had found on the floor, Sheila was certain he was going to use it to beat her, but when she asked him what he planned to do with it, Ice tossed it back onto the floor.

But that didn't stop him only minutes later from grabbing a soda bottle and beating her about the face and head, while little Donna stood there watching in horror. When the blood began running down Sheila's face, Ice permitted the little girl to leave the room to get a wash cloth and clean her mother's face. During this time, Ice again began to address the air, declaring how he couldn't believe Sheila had not been knocked out by his savage beating, and how "it was all so easy to begin with." And it was perhaps at this time Ice, in a great fit of anger, broke the canopy post of Donna's bed.

The "it" Ice referred to was his decision to use violence the moment he was confronted by their return. Even so, he must have been somewhat confused as to what exactly he should do and when he should do it. Authorities later calculated that Ice remained in the Knox residence at least two hours, and because he could have easily brought them inside and killed them immediately but didn't, he spent a considerable amount of time figuring out just what to do. And while some people believe Todd Ice went to the Knox's that evening with the intent of committing murder, the thought to kill may have come in a flash, and since he had no compunction against committing such a deed, he acted upon it.

In Sheila's mind, however, there was little doubt what the outcome would be from the very moment she felt the blade of the kitchen knife being plunged into her back. Particularly distressing was her concern for Donna and what the disturbed young man might do to her. One can easily imagine the terror and confusion little Donna Knox experienced, for not only was she forced to watch Ice as he was beating her mother, she also had to helplessly stand back as he attempted to suffocate her as well. Yet, just as the beating failed to render Sheila unconscious, Ice also failed in his suffocation attempt, and he soon retreated to the living room.

Donna, who'd been constantly at her mother's side wiping her swollen face, now stopped and said she needed to use the bathroom. At the same time her daughter was talking to her, Sheila could hear the familiar sound of her husband's rifle case being unzipped. Seconds later, Ice entered the room and immediately began beating her on the side and back of her head with the rifle butt, thus causing her to pass out. He then unsheathed his hunting knife and started slashing her throat; a move, he believed, that would finally kill the obstinate and seemingly indestructible woman. Believing Sheila Knox was dead, Ice attacked Donna while she was still in the bathroom, beating her about the head, stabbing her, and finally cutting her throat. According to police reports, Donna was found lying in a large pool of blood on the bathroom floor, her head being nearly decapitated.

By the time Todd Ice left the Knox trailer, his family had already formed a search party and was out looking for him. December 5, 1978, had begun quite normally for the Ice household. When the kids returned home from school, Mrs. Ice took them to a Christmas-play practice in nearby Stanton, Kentucky, which did not end until 6 p.m. or a little later. She then returned home to tell Todd to do his chores and she was taking his brother Scott to a ballgame. On the drive over, however, Mrs. Ice decided it was getting too late and headed home, but first she stopped at a donut shop. Back at the house, Mrs. Ice told her son to help Todd with the chores, and she had another errand to make. She promised to return home soon. But when Dana called home just a short time later, Scott said Todd was nowhere to be found. This frightened Mrs. Ice, who raced home so they could begin searching for him.

At first, it was just Dana and Scott wandering about, but after looking for awhile without seeing any sign of Todd, they returned home and telephoned Anna Benningfield, asking if she could bring a flashlight and help in the search. She did, along with Jana Benningfield and twenty-year-old Raymond Elam. No sooner had the party started searching they saw Todd standing in the middle of a bridge. Dana immediately ran to her son and demanded to know where he'd been. Todd, obviously frightened, told her a man with a beard had held him at gunpoint in the woods, and he'd heard them calling out to him but was too afraid to answer.

Taking Todd at his word, fear now gripped the little band and they decided to head back to the Ice's trailer to call the Sheriff's Department. While Dana contacted the police Scott ran to the Knox trailer to warn them about the "bearded man." Scott pounded on the trailer door, but as no one answered, he returned home. When Raymond Elam heard this, he went back to the Knox's trailer "to warn Sheila." This time, however, the knocking on the door produced an unintelligible sound from somewhere inside. Raymond Elam then ran back to the Ice residence.

Apparently, fear had gotten the better part of the search party as they quickly turned off all the lights while waiting for the police to arrive, evidently believing "the man from the woods" would be deterred from entering and killing them all.

Officer Cephus Allen was the first person to arrive at the Knox residence. Entering, he found the body of Donna on the bathroom floor. When he located Sheila, she was able to tell him that her neighbor, Todd Ice, had done this to them. According to the autopsy report, Ice had beaten Donna with such force that when Deputy Coroner Carl Walls examined her, he observed four distinct indentations in her forehead.

When Officer Allen returned to the Ice home, he informed Mrs. Ice that "the lady in the trailer said Todd Ice was the one that done this." Although Allen had said nothing about the murder, Todd Ice blurted out, "I didn't kill anyone." As Todd stood there proclaiming his innocence, Officer Allen noticed blood stains on Todd's jeans and what appeared to be blood-spatter on his boots and jacket. Todd Ice was immediately given his rights and placed under arrest.

For the most part, the case against Ice was rock-solid, at least as far as the police were concerned. Yet it was destined to "play out" like any ordinary capital murder case, although this was no ordinary killing. The accused, a fifteen-year-old boy, void of any criminal record, a church camp counselor, and member of the 4H club, was being charged with one of the most heinous crimes possible: The killing of a child.

Just one week after the murder, on December 12, Dr. Maria Pinho performed, in what would be the first of two meetings, a psychiatric evaluation on Ice. In Pinho's report are some very enlightening observations concerning Todd's personality, observations where one can easily draw correlations between the murder and something of which Todd was very proud: "He is proudest of the prizes he won at the state fair on his insect collection. Apparently, his father also used to collect insects, and Todd had been doing that. He told me with quite a bit of emotion for Todd, that when he cuts the insects he puts them in a jar where they are coated with some kind of chemical, and then when he closes the jar he says that the fumes strangle the insects. It is interesting, though, that both the child died because she was cut in the throat and the mother was partially strangled and also had her neck slashed." Concluding her five- page report, Dr. Pinho wrote: "It seems to me that Todd has been operating, using a great deal of reaction formation and, therefore, his personality is not well integrated. There is a great deal of anger, anxiety, and confusion that has been controlled but not dealt with. If for some reason there is a breakthrough on his control mechanisms, a great deal of anger can emerge and it will be impossible for Todd to contain it." In layman's terms, Ice was a walking time bomb.

It is also interesting to note, that when Dr. Pinho asked him what he regretted most in his life, he said it was giving up playing basketball in school. Finding this more than a little odd, she added: "Usually, when I ask youngsters about what they regret in life, the response is that they did something that was mischievous or somewhat delinquent. Therefore, his answer was rather unusual."

But Dr. Pinho was not the only medical expert to evaluate Todd Ice. In all, four individuals peered deeply into the life of this young killer. And, as can be expected, opinions varied among the doctors as to what his state of mind was during the murder, and what was his mental condition now that he was under their care. Terms like, "paranoid psychosis," "schizophrenic," "psychotic breaks," were tossed about in an attempt to explain why a fifteen-year-old boy would commit such a crime.

Dr. Robert J.G. Lang suggested that any subsequent psychosis Todd had experienced might have derived from, "after stress factors." Ice's attorneys were hoping their client would be diagnosed as insane – both during and after the murder – but such a diagnosis did not come. Neither did they get their wish that Todd be tried as a juvenile. In the Court's ruling that Ice should be tried as an adult, the record states: "This court…finds that it is in the best interest of the juvenile, Todd Ice, and the community, to order the transfer of this cause to the Powell circuit court for disposition under the laws governing adults. This finding is based upon the court's acknowledgement that the offense committed to Donna Knox was in fact the most serious in that a human life was taken and the lifes (sic) of many shattered by the tragedy."

The Court, fully realizing its limited ability to dispense justice in this case, added: "No law applicable can ever open the eyes of the slain youth, but it is this court's opinion that such a horrendous, brutal offense should not be left for disposition in a system that cannot adequately punish the wrong doer if found guilty." And speaking of punishment, had Todd Ice not been locked away so tightly, being continually squeezed between the medical teams and the justice system, there was the very real fear that the enraged folks of Powell County would exact some form of frontier justice from Donna's killer. Indeed, eight days after the murder, the Ice home was torched and burned to the ground, and the Ice family was driven "out of the county at gunpoint." Even the police were concerned. Kentucky State Police Officer "Babe" Howard testified in court that "there's really high sentiment in this case…normally people will control (themselves) to the point there's no harm done, but in this particular case, I wouldn't say that for a fact." And he warned "of what could happen should this boy be back in Powell County." When a police detective was questioned as to how bad the situation was, he responded, "You really can't imagine."

Because of the volatile nature of the case, the defense requested and was granted a change of venue for the trial, but only to neighboring Wolf County. This was unacceptable to the defense, but further protests were fruitless, and trial commenced in September 1980. Lead prosecutor for the Commonwealth of Kentucky, Dale Bryant, began his opening statement by focusing on the Knox family and how quickly the flame of little Donna's life was extinguished. Using the metaphor of an hourglass, he said: "Sly Knox and his wife Sheila, and their only child Donna, who lived seven years, three months, twenty days, and fifteen minutes..."

Accompanying the prosecution was a picture of Donna, taken in happier times. Ice's attorney, Clyde Simmons, objected to the picture being displayed, saying the picture was of "the deceased little girl sitting on this lovely bed in her night cloths with a little doll dressed approximately like her sitting next to her." Evidently, they believed the picture was intended to "inflame and enrage the jury" Simmons was overruled. But Bryant wasn't finished. Much to the dismay of the defense team, Bryant also displayed pictures of Donna lying dead on the coroner's table. Of course, these images, when comparing the image with that of the living little girl, were designed to make the viewer cringe. Again, Simmons objected but was overruled.

For Dale Bryant, the facts of this case were clear, and it was his intention to build a solid one against the homicidal youth. As he concluded his opening statement, he again focused on the Knoxes and their life without Donna: "The Knox family moved ...into their new home, but they moved in alone, because Donna was all they had, and she missed Christmas that year, because she was in the graveyard."

When Simmons presented his case to the jury, he told them he would prove Donna was killed - not by their client - but by a friend of Todd's, a boy named Gavin Madison (a pseudonym). It seems Madison had confessed to the murder several times. He later recanted, saying he'd been with his mother the entire night Donna was killed. A polygraph test was administered to Madison and his mother, and the results were consistent with Gavin having told the truth about not being involved in the crime. When Simmons found out about the polygraph, apparently during the discovery phase of the trial, he fought to keep it from being admitted as evidence but was unsuccessful. When asked why he would confess to a crime he didn't commit, Madison said he believed it would "increase his stature in the eyes of other inmates, and to make the staff scared of him."

Gavin Madison was not only a known drug user, but he'd been referred to as a "wind bag" by some, and it's doubtful that anyone who knew him believed he'd murdered Donna. And besides, Sheila Knox lived to identify her attacker. Even so, the defense kept pounding away that Madison was the killer and Todd Ice was insane at the time of the crime. This was a tactic designed to help Ice, should the jury fail to believe Madison murdered the girl but could be swayed into believing Ice murdered her while insane. If this ploy was successful he could be found not guilty "by reason of insanity."

Yet it would take the jury only thirty minutes to find

Ice guilty of the murder of Donna Knox. During the sentencing phase of the trial, held several days later, Judge Graham summed up what was probably the feeling in all of Powell County:

"I have never known any defendant in any case who could apparently derive pleasure out of killing and torturing a small child. I am convinced that on that rainy day on the 5th of December, 1978, that the defendant took that knife and went over there and broke into that trailer and intended to wipe out their whole family." It took the jury little more than one hour to hand down a sentence of death, making the now sixteen-year-old, the youngest person on death row.

But Ice would be waiting for the executioner only so long. Donna had been in the cemetery in Stanton, Kentucky only three years, when the Kentucky Supreme Court overturned his conviction, citing various errors committed by the prosecution and the judge, thereby ensuring a new trial for defendant. And it would be during this second trial, in 1986, that Ice would be convicted of the lesser crime of manslaughter. Apparently, his attorneys, Kevin McNally and Gail Robinson (who were husband and wife) were able to establish a pattern of mental illness that ran in the Ice family, including Todd, and they were able to convince the jury their client committed the murder while in a state of "extreme emotional disturbance." And from their perspective, the subsequent conviction of manslaughter was a victory for Ice, as it plucked him forever out of the unforgiving hands of death row. And like the proverbial icing on the cake, it meant the maximum penalty their client could receive was twenty years in prison, part of which he'd already served, making him immediately eligible for parole.

In due course, McNally and Robinson, who truly believed Ice deserved treatment for his mental illness, pressed the parole board to place him within the psychiatric system for monitoring and therapy. But thirteen thousand signatures from irate residents of eastern Kentucky carried more weight with the parole board, and they flatly rejected that idea. Instead, Ice would serve the remainder of his sentence behind bars.

Over the next couple of years, his attorneys would often visit him in prison. On numerous occasions, they would bring their young son along to spend time with the incarcerated child-killer, who patiently taught the boy how to play chess while the parents watched how well the two of them got along. And not long after this, when they were convinced Ice's illness had gone into remission, they considered allowing him to live with them in their home after his release.

Soon after this, however, Ice descended into an even darker place where he refused to bath himself or keep his cell clean. At his lowest point he slashed his arm with a razor and started a fire in his cell. His true madness was now being unmasked. And by 1990, Ice began striking out at his attorneys through letters that promised torture and death should that become necessary. According to brief excerpts of these letters published in *The Courier-Journal*, Ice told Robinson: "I will kill without regret again if the circumstances merit it." To McNally he wrote: "Everything that you, your wife, and your children have is at stake... and that includes all the emotional and physical pain your bodies can produce." Perhaps most disturbing was his reference to an internal struggle: "You do not understand what I had to do to become someone who does not cut the throats of little girls."

Robinson reluctantly released the contents of these letters just prior to Ice's parole, hoping that the-powers-that-be would be made aware of how dangerous it was to release Ice back into the general public. And so, on March 11, 1994, a mental inquest trial was held in Jefferson Circuit Court in Louisville to determine whether Ice posed a danger to himself or others. For some, like Dr. Nolker, Ice was just as dangerous today as he was when he slit the throat of Donna Knox. To others, like psychiatric social worker, Gail Johnson, Ice was not "psychotic," and shouldn't be detained in any mental institution against his will. Yet the decision to set Ice free was not up to any of his doctors or social workers, but to a jury of six in a trial where the judge took the unusual step of opening up the proceedings to the public.

As was mentioned earlier, Robinson and McNally wanted to help Ice by having him committed against his will, thereby forcing him to receive the treatment they believed he so desperately needed, and at the same time, they'd be protecting the public. The current Ice defense team, however, saw things differently, declaring such information as "stale, irrelevant, and highly prejudicial."

Andrew Wolfson, a reporter with *The Courier-Journal*, pointed out one of the greatest ironies in the saga of Todd Ice when he wrote: "While his lawyers at his two criminal trials contended Ice was insane, his present attorneys will try to prove he is not mentally ill." For a brief period, sanity would reign as Todd Ice was committed to a mental hospital for the next 360 days. When this term expired, Ice voluntarily continued his treatment, but other commitments would follow, and it soon became clear to all that keeping Todd Ice permanently locked up against his will would be virtually impossible. It also didn't help matters that some of the doctors working with Ice believed he was making real progress, and that under Kentucky law, a person can only be involuntarily committed if he poses a real danger to himself or others. And because Ice had always been a "model" patient, it would only be a matter of time before he would no longer meet their criteria for confinement.

To almost everyone else in the state of Kentucky, the thought that Todd Ice would ever be allowed to walk the streets again was unthinkable. In the eyes of many, justice was denied when Ice escaped the electric chair, and now to hear of his possible release was like a slap in the face to all that is rational. Dr. Nolker's feeling on the matter, as quoted in *The Courier-Journal*, left little to the imagination: "The tragedy in the case of Todd Ice is that somebody else is going to die. We just don't know where or when."

The news of Ice's release came quietly, in March of

1996, when it was discovered he was living in a half-way house in Covington, Kentucky, a city along the Ohio River directly across from Cincinnati, Ohio. No one bothered to inform the Covington Police Department that a child-killer was now living among them, for as a mental patient, Todd Ice had certain rights under the law, and one of those rights was the right to privacy. Yet, when Covington Police Chief Bill Dorsey was interviewed by Steve Croft, of CBS's *60 Minutes*, he was clearly disturbed that such a thing could have occurred: "People want to be safe. We have smoke detectors for our house. We have warning labels on the back of cigarettes and alcohol. And yet we hesitate to warn the public about the worst predator of all on this globe, which is man." Public outcry against Ice was swift. Even the Governor was deluged with calls from angry citizens, and soon Ice was whisked away from Covington, as this first attempt at giving Ice his life back failed miserably.

On October 4, 1996, health officials announced Todd Ice had been moved out of Kentucky. Where he was placed was a closely guarded secret. And just like Covington, Kentucky, wherever Todd Ice was placed, it's fairly certain those who passed him on the street or sat next to him on a bus or in a restaurant had no idea what he was. They probably took little notice of him. Even so, the years following his release brought no new news of the slaughter of any other little girls, and, apparently, Todd Ice was able to keep any bad impulses in check as he navigated each of his days.

Then, on October 21, 2010, which ironically was his forty-seventh birthday, Todd Ice died of a heart attack.   When news of his death circulated among those who lived through the ordeal of the murder of little Donna Knox, many breathed a sigh of relief.

A WORM IN THE NOSE

Exactly when things started to go wrong in the life of James R. Becker no one knows for sure, but by 1984, his family had little doubt he was a very sick young man and in need of professional help. Coming into the world on July 4, 1959, James Becker was the first of three children born to Ray and Barbara Becker. Soon a brother and sister followed, and it appears the family lived quite happily, at least for the first few years of the marriage. But at some point, trouble began to surface in the relationship, and when James was twelve, Ray and Barbara Becker filed for divorce. Two years later, Becker's mother married Thomas A. Rankin, the grandson of Doctor Charles H. Mayo, founder of the world famous Mayo Clinic. At no time during the divorce of his parents, or throughout his formative teenage years, did James Becker exhibit any signs of mental instability. Indeed, it would be years before anything would rise to sound the alarm in the Rankin home concerning the mental health of James.

According to Becker's mother's later testimony, young James was a quiet and shy boy, a boy she always considered "kind, caring, and gentle." Of course, such a personality can be a hindrance, especially when one needs to stand up for oneself if the situation arises. As such, upon hearing that a particular kid at school had been picking on James, she instructed him to punch out the boy the next time he started to pick a fight. Being an obedient son, James did as his mother asked and broke his hand in the process.

Concerning his feelings for his stepfather, Barbara Rankin spoke of a warm relationship between the two, at least for the first few years. In fact, Becker often referred to Thomas Rankin as "dad," and Mr. Rankin was so impressed with how things were going, he mentioned to his wife that he planned to leave James an extra ten-thousand dollars in his will. Unfortunately, things began to cool between them when Rankin's natural born son noticed the closeness and began to complain openly about it to his father. According to Mrs. Rankin's sworn testimony, it was at this time her husband started to withdraw somewhat from James, and as she remembered it, "Tom was trying to be loyal to his son and trying to please the both of them."

Still, none of this sparked any outward anger or violent reactions within James Becker. Indeed, the remainder of his teenager years proceeded quite normally. Only gradually did those around him begin seeing certain traits that gave one pause.

"He graduated from high school and was engaged and he went out and got a job," remembered Barbara Rankin. "He saved money and bought a house trailer…he bought a brand new pick-up truck, and he was paying for all of this himself. And then within a very short period of time, his girlfriend broke off the engagement, and he lost his job at Rand McNally, and the truck, when it was maybe two months old, was stolen from right outside his door. It was found four years later in Whitley County in the possession of an ex-sheriff."

Another blow occurred during the winter of 1983 when Becker lost his job at a trucking company after the company was sold. At this time, he turned to his mother and stepfather, asking to be employed on their farm in Nicholasville, Kentucky. "He asked if he could work for us…and we said fine, and he started working for us, but he was increasingly having trouble sleeping at night."

During this time, Becker was allowed to live on his parents' property, but he was often restless and afraid, believing people were coming onto the farm at night, breaking into his trailer and beating him, adding that as many as one hundred people could be on the farm at any given time. He also told his mother someone was driving the tractor through the fields - presumably by the same people - in addition to their other nocturnal activities. Yet the madness did not end here.

Becker also believed his stepfather had placed a worm in his nose, and this worm had made its way into his brain, and it was the cause of all of his current troubles. Becker also said other family members were urinating in his ears while he slept, and his sister, who was experiencing vision problems, wanted to steal his eyes. He would also tell of having special powers that allowed him to tap into radio and television signals at will. As if all of this wasn't enough, Becker informed his family he was also part wolf.

Of course, as any normal family would attempt to do, they tried to reason with him, but it proved to be an impossible task. Even when Becker was shown he was incorrect about certain oddities of which he believed, like the time he told them the world would end on his birthday, he just shrugged it off.

The year 1984 saw the first of several hospitalizations for Becker, who was diagnosed a paranoid schizophrenic. And while such a diagnosis is indeed terrible, it does not automatically mean the individual will become violent. But the threat of violence was a very real concern for the Rankins who understood that anything was possible in such situations. When Barbara Rankin once asked her son whether he could become violent, Becker answered no, declaring he had never and would never hurt anyone. And perhaps James really did believe what he was saying, but this didn't stop him from making threats against Thomas Rankin, whom he promised to scare to death.

There were times, of course, when Becker's personality improved while on the anti-psychotic medications. Yet when he failed to take his medication as prescribed (and Barbara Rankin could always tell when her son skipped doses), he would become far more paranoid and generally unstable. So, it must have been a great relief to the Rankins when in late 1984, Becker began living with another mental patient in an apartment in Lexington, Kentucky. And while he was still permitted to visit them at the farm, they told him he could only come during daylight hours. No night visits were allowed. And the Rankins took an extra precaution: they began locking their bedroom door at night.

If only all of this worked.

Early on the morning of June 27, 1985, James Becker arrived at the farm and was met by Thomas Rankin who had just retrieved the morning paper from the newspaper box out by the road. As Barbara Rankin would later tell police, as her husband walked back into the house he "called up the stairs to me and said Jimmy was there and wanted to talk with me...I went downstairs, and the two of them were sitting in the den, and we visited for a little bit, and then I went into the kitchen to fix breakfast." Mrs. Rankin invited her son to join them for the morning meal, but James declined, saying he'd already eaten donuts. Barbara Rankin also mentioned she'd noticed her son seemed a little nervous. As the two of them talked in the kitchen, Mr. Rankin remained in the den, not knowing he now had only minutes to live.

Barbara Rankin continued talking with her son for

several more minutes, until James told her he needed to get something from his truck. Before he could walk out the door, she asked him to take out the trash. He complied. Moments later, Mrs. Rankin heard an odd noise coming from the den. When she raced into the room, she found her husband lying on the floor, with an arrowhead protruding from his back. He was completely unresponsive and, in fact, died within seconds of being shot. The type of arrowhead used in the attack is known as a Broadhead, properly configured for large animals, such as deer or bear. According to the pathology report: "Mr. Thomas A. Rankin died as a result of a perforating sharp force injury (arrow wound) of the trunk, with massive internal hemorrhage. The arrow pierced the right and left ventricles of the heart, left lower lobe of the lung, and superior pole of the spleen producing massive internal hemorrhage." As Barbara Rankin first entered the den to view the terrible sight, she caught a glimpse of Becker from the window as he walked to his truck.

James Bishop, who was married to Becker's sister and lived and worked on the farm, watched Becker drive away, not knowing what had transpired in the house only moments before. Bishop would later testify that Becker did not seem to be in a hurry as he drove away and actually waved at him as he passed him. Within seconds, however, Bishop heard the screams of Mrs. Rankin and ran the two hundred yards to the house. Another farmhand, who'd also heard her cries, followed him. Once inside, Bishop found the deceased lying on his side, not far from the blood-spattered door Thomas Rankin had been standing next to when he was shot. After grabbing a bolt cutter, Bishop cut off the arrowhead and part of the shaft sticking out of Thomas Rankin's back, and the tail portion sticking out of his chest.

How odd this must have seemed to James Bishop, for like Becker, he too had a compound bow, and the two of them used to spend time shooting arrows for fun while on the farm.

When police arrived from the Nicholasville Police Department, the sheriff's department, and the Kentucky State Police, they were met by a distraught widow who told them who'd killed her husband, and what life was like living under the threats of her mentally ill son. She also said James might be heading to his brother's house in Anderson County. Nicholasville PD then notified their counterparts in the area, and shortly thereafter, Kentucky State Police officers, out of Frankfort, located James Becker on KY 144 near the Spencer County line. In all, Becker's flight from the crime scene did not exceed thirty miles before he was apprehended. When Becker exited the vehicle, he was holding a soft drink in his hand, and as the officers kept their weapons trained on him, he was instructed to put the can on the ground, and get face down on the pavement. Instead, Becker decided to sit on the ground. As he was being handcuffed, he told officers he'd killed his stepfather and would do it again. Sergeant John Witt quickly advised him to stop talking and read him his constitutional rights.

Because of James Becker's mental condition, it

would be two years before he'd be judged competent to stand trial. When this did occur, on January 20, 1987, there was no shortage of people willing to tell of Becker's insanity, or at least his severe mental illness preceding the killing of Thomas Rankin. Those given the task of defending Becker were eager to have him declared not guilty by reason of insanity; an outcome the prosecution was desperately trying to avoid. And apparently, attorneys for the Commonwealth of Kentucky did their job well, as the jury returned a verdict of guilty, but mentally ill.

During the sentencing phase of the trial, the jury recommended a ten-year prison term. And while Becker's time in physical confinement would be relatively short, the prison of his illness would be something else altogether.

CLOSING TIME

The evening of January 7, 1981, was extremely cold. By 8 p.m., the temperature in Louisville was hovering around the eight-degree mark, and Barbel (pronounced "Babble", according to court records) Poore, a twenty-year-old single mother of an eleven-month-old girl, was working as an attendant at the Checker Oil station at 4501 Cane Run Road. It was not unusual for her to be working alone, and perhaps she believed that closing the station at the relatively early hour of eight o'clock would not prove to be a danger. Still, it wasn't the safest neighborhood, and she would work to get the job completed in a timely fashion.

At approximately 7:55 p.m., Ingrid Poore telephoned her daughter, but Barbel, who was shutting down and auditing the pumps, told her mother she was too busy to talk. The two ended their conversation, and Barbel returned to her duties.

Minutes earlier, Barbel Poore had gone out to the car her mother had loaned her, started it, and pulled it up to the front door, allowing it to warm up while she finished doing the paperwork. A few minutes after making her first call, her mother again called Barbel to ask her if she'd purchased the car she had looked at earlier in the day. These would be the last words mother and daughter would ever say to one another. Perhaps within seconds of hanging up the phone, Barbel watched as two teenagers - one of whom was carrying a handgun - walked through the front door. The individual holding the pistol, seventeen-year-old Kevin Nigel Stanford, who lived in the Oakwood apartments next door to the Checker station, knew Barbel Poore and had even spoken to her and her parents on several occasions. Yet, in true psychopathic fashion, Stanford, along with sixteen-year-old David Buchanan, attacked the young woman. Within a minute or so of entering the gas station, the men raped, and orally and anally sodomized Barbel, while an accomplice (also a juvenile) waited outside in a car.

The attack, which occurred on the station's bathroom floor, lasted up to forty-five minutes. According to court records, after Barbel was led into the bathroom, she was forced to remove her shoes, socks, jeans, and panties. Although much of the assault would take place on the floor, at one point, Barbel was raped from behind as she bent over and held onto the wash basin; a fact later discovered as members of the Evidence Unit located her prints on both sides of the basin.

At some point during the attack, Buchanan returned to the vehicle and gave the driver a two-gallon, gas can, filled to the top with gasoline just stolen from the station, and told him to stay in the car. Soon after this, Buchanan again returned and told him that he and Stanford were going to continue having sex with Poore, but not at the station. Kevin Stanford then drove Poore in her mother's car to a secluded area on Shanks Lane, only several blocks away and within sight of her place of employment, stopping the vehicle in the middle of the road between Obe Lane and the railroad tracks. Buchanan and the other juvenile rolled up minutes later behind Ingrid Poore's dark-green, 1973 Chevrolet Impala and switched off the lights.

Buchanan then walked over to Stanford, who was standing beside their captive's car. Over the next few minutes, Barbel Poore, who was sitting in the back seat, was forced to pull down her pants and panties, which were left dangling around her ankles. She was then forced to assume a kneeling position, with her face directed toward the left rear of the vehicle, exposing her buttocks to further, unwanted assaults. Ingrid Poore, unable to reach her daughter by phone, stopped by the Checker station on her way home from work, arriving there at approximately 11:45 p.m. A quick look around told her something was amiss: The pumps were still turned on even though Barbel had told her mother that she was in the process of shutting them down; the station was in "disarray," and, worst of all, Barbel was nowhere to be found. The frightened mother immediately called police.

At 12:42 a.m., a police cruiser driving down Shanks Lane came upon a vehicle sitting in the middle of the snowy road; its lights switched off. A check of the license plate number showed it to be registered to Ingrid Poore. The officer approaching the vehicle was unable to see what or who might be inside the Impala, due to frost covering the windows. Once the door was popped open, however, a terrible sight awaited him: "Barbel Poore's corpse was left kneeling in the backseat of her mother's car, naked from the waist down with her buttocks elevated." She had been shot once in the side of the face, and once through the skull, leaving a large pool of blood surrounding her head. The Evidence Technician Unit was called to the scene, and those responsible for gathering the crucial evidence did so methodically until dawn. Afterward, the remains of Barbel Poore were transferred to the University of Louisville Hospital for a post-mortem examination. According to her autopsy report and other related court documents, the young mother suffered terribly before she was finally killed: "Injuries to the victim's anus included a contusion 'with radiating abrasions over the anal mucous over the entire circumferential surface' inside of which were 'large quantities of spermatozoa.'" An additional report reveals: "Anal contusions and abrasions with severe contusion on the left side of her anus. Motile spermatozoa were present in anal swabs and in fixed anal swabs... spermatozoa was present in her mouth and in her vagina."

The reports also reveal the damage caused by the bullets, and which shot resulted in her death:"Penetrating non-contact gunshot wound measuring .5x.5 centimeters on the on the right side of head approximately 2 inches above the ear with brain lacerations and skull fractures on the right side. The bullet lodged in the brain cavity and death was due to this wound. Penetrating non-contact gunshot measuring .7x.8 centimeters to the right side of the face with oral mucous membrane lacerations and mandibular (sic) fractures. The bullet traveled downward from the mouth, fractured her teeth, pierced her tongue and lodged at C2 on the right side of the neck."

It was clear to authorities that whoever murdered Barbel Poore, made little or no attempt to clean up the crime scene or remove any items such as clothing, which might contain evidence. Of the clothing removed from the body of Poore, the report said the following: "A ' large volume of semen' was found on the left sleeve, front and back hem of her outer jacket, on her inner jacket, on her sweater, on her panties, and on the back seat of her mother's car where Barbel's head laid." (The semen found near the head was no doubt residue that dripped out of her mouth after death occurred.)

Pubic and head hairs removed from Barbel's buttocks, left thigh, jacket, other articles of clothing, and from the back seat of her mother's car, told police the perpetrators were two African-Americans, which was true. After their arrests, police would link which hairs matched "in color and microscopic characteristics" to David Buchanan, and which matched to Kevin Stanford. And something else was discovered on the inside the vehicle where Barbel was killed: Kevin Stanford's fingerprint.

On January 9, 1981, the Louisville Police Intelligence Unit contacted Detective Jerry Hall, informing him of two individuals who were selling cigarettes identified as having been stolen from the Checker station. Police were aware some three hundred cartons of cigarettes had been taken the night Barbel was killed: "Later that night, (the night of the murder) a neighbor named Alexis Sloan saw Stanford carrying two large boxes of cartons of cigarettes away from the Checker station. Sloan agreed to 'hold' the cigarettes for Stanford. The following day, Sloan, and one Darren Smith (a pseudonym) put the cigarettes into plastic garbage bags and roamed about the neighborhood selling them. Afterwards, Stanford told Sloan the cigarettes were from the Checker station and that he had made a play for them."

Although Sloan was apparently willing to help Stanford unload the cigarettes, once he learned about the murder of Barbel Poore, neither he nor Smith wanted anything to do with them. At the same time, police were receiving information concerning Kevin Stanford's involvement in the crime, and on January 13, he was brought in to Jefferson County Police Headquarters for questioning. Stanford's attorney intervened and demanded police either charge his client or release him. As authorities were not yet ready to press charges, they decided to let him go. However, later that evening, Stanford was arrested, and according to court records, gave a taped statement to police, implicating not David Buchanan, but Calvin Buchanan, David's uncle. Calvin Buchanan was then arrested, and while protesting his innocence, asked permission to call his nephew, and suggested police tape the conversation. Detectives agreed, and soon David would be heard admitting his involvement "at the Checker station." A search of Stanford's grandmother's apartment at 4507 Cane Run Road, where Kevin Stanford was living, produced a set of keys belonging to the Checker station. The murder weapon was soon recovered at another location, as was the two-gallon, gas can.

As the investigation began to take shape, along with the evidence, the statements made by David Buchanan and Kevin Stanford would all be tied nicely together by the juvenile accomplice, who, while admitting he drove the car that evening, did not participate in the sexual assault and subsequent murder. He also agreed to testify against his friends. And from this came the "how" and "why" this deadly trio decided to invade the Checker station on that cold, winter night.

Sometime that afternoon, David Buchanan asked his friend if he wanted to rob the Checker station, but his friend said no. Not wanting to hear this, Buchanan said that robbing the station would be "easy" and that no one would get hurt. This time the friend agreed, and even provided Buchanan with a revolver he'd taken from his brother's room. And then, "Buchanan telephoned Stanford in regard to the plan. The three met at Stanford's apartment, then proceeded to the Checker station where the juvenile remained inside the getaway car. As Stanford was leaving to go inside the Checker station, he expressed concern… that the victim might recognize him by his clothing."

As described earlier, once the sexual assault at the station ended, Stanford drove Barbel in her mother's car to Shanks Lane, with Buchanan and the juvenile arriving minutes later. The following is taken from a document contained within the Kentucky Supreme Court record: "After both cars arrived at a secluded area on Shanks Lane in Louisville, Buchanan got out of (the juvenile's) car and walked over to the victim's car where Stanford was standing.

Prior to executing her, Stanford allowed Barbel Poore to smoke a last cigarette. Instead of having further sex with her, Stanford leaned inside the victim's car and shot her in the face at point-blank range. At that point (the juvenile) got out of his car, poured the stolen gas into his gas tank, got back into his vehicle and started the engine, and began backing up. Stanford then fired a second shot into the back of the victim's head, causing her death."

Both Kevin Stanford and David Buchanan were tried as adults. And while police were already convinced that Stanford was the one responsible for firing the shots that killed Barbel Poore, they received some unexpected help from Kevin Stanford himself. While being held in jail, Stanford, in a bizarre move, walked up behind a guard, put a pencil to the back of the guard's ear, and said, "Click, click, click, just like the girl, I'm going to blow your mother…brains out." And, to another corrections officer he said, "I had to shoot her, the bitch lived next door to me, and she would recognize me…I guess we could have tied her up or something or beat the piss out of her and tell her, if she tell [sic], we would kill her." As such, it came as little surprise to those who followed the case through the newspapers or by television, when Kevin Stanford was convicted of the sexual assault and murder of Barbel Poore and sentenced to death. David Buchanan was also convicted of murdering and assaulting Barbel Poore, but because he didn't fire the weapon, he was spared the death penalty. Instead, he was given a sentence of life, plus sixty-years for his crimes.

Kevin Stanford languished on death row for many years. Each appeal presented by his attorneys was struck down by the courts; even the United States Supreme Court refused to reverse the decisions of the lower courts. Time was running out for the killer, when, in July of 2003, out-going governor, Paul Patton, made good on a promise to commute the death sentence of Kevin Stanford. Apparently he believed he was "righting a wrong," as he later stated to the media, because the killer had committed the sexual assault/murder when he was only seventeen.

Kevin Stanford is now serving a life sentence without the possibility of parole.

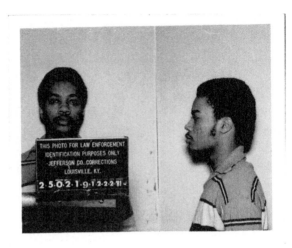

*Appearing to smirk, Kevin Stanford is booked for the sexual
assault and murder of Barbal Poore*

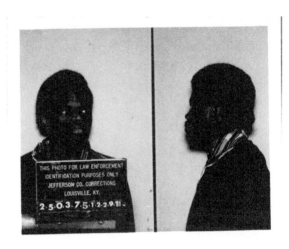

David Buchanan, the accomplice of Kevin Stanford

Murder site of Barbal Poore, just beyond the railroad tracks

THE BEST OF FRIENDS

In the early morning hours of September 30, 1984, Louisville Police Officer Mel Allen, while on routine patrol, noticed a blue "newer model, and in good condition" Datsun, parked at a deserted lot at 318 Ardella Court in downtown Louisville. Ardella Court, which in reality is nothing more than an alleyway running between Floyd and Preston streets, had, at the time, a number of abandoned and boarded up houses, and a large weed-covered lot. Naturally, seeing a nice vehicle sitting in such an area aroused his suspicions. When Officer Allen ran the registration, the dispatcher radioed back the vehicle had not been reported stolen, and was registered "to an address in the 1600 block of Sylvan," an address many miles away, and a much better area than where the car was now sitting.

As patrolman Allen continued making his rounds through the darkened alleyways and well-lit streets of the neighborhoods south of downtown Louisville, he began thinking about the Datsun practically hidden away on Ardella Court. Radioing fellow officer, Pat Willis, who'd traveled the same beat covering Ardella Court the night before, Allen asked if he'd seen the Datsun during last night's patrol. Willis answered that he may have seen it, or a car like it, but he couldn't remember if it was on Ardella or Airmont, which was one block further south. The two decided to rendezvous on Ardella Court, but as soon as Officer Willis saw the vehicle, he told Allen it was not the same car. After contacting the dispatcher and signing themselves off the air, Allen and Willis began searching the weed-covered field adjacent to the lot where the Datsun was parked. It was now 3:05 a.m.

At 2:25 a.m., Donata Nelson was lying in bed, listening to her police scanner (a practice that had become quite a habit for her over the years). Recorded in an interview she and her husband Emory gave to Louisville Police detectives the next day, she became concerned after hearing her address being given by the dispatcher in response to a license registration check. "I have a police scanner that I listen to at night," she told detectives "that puts me to sleep…if you can believe that! I listen to all the awful things that go on, but anyway, all of a sudden I woke up… and then what I heard was the dispatcher…saying 1614 Sylvan Way; on a Datsun, no color given." Alarmed, Donata Nelson ran into the living room to tell her husband what she'd just heard. "And we assumed," the report said "that Scott (their son) had gotten stopped somewhere and was speeding or something…and was getting a ticket."

Earlier that evening, between 7:30 and 7:45 p.m., seventeen-year-old Scott Nelson left his home to pick up his best friend, Richard David Stephenson, also seventeen, as the two had plans to attend a football game between their school, Trinity, and rival Manuel High School in downtown Louisville. Being students at Trinity High, located in the eastern portion of Jefferson County, they were not familiar with the area they were entering and had only a general idea where Manuel High School was located. To make matters worse, they were unaware that Manuel didn't play their home games at the actual high school, but at a stadium about a mile away. Later, police would learn how hard they tried to find their way to the school and what had happened in the process.

Detective Sharon Weston, in her report of September 30, 1984, describes the result of the search of the weed-covered lot on Ardella Court: "He (Allen) states that they began shinning their flashlights south of where the vehicle was parked, and that their flashlights hit something white. He said that upon walking and getting a closer view, they observed (two) bodies, and…at this point, he and Officer Willis backed off, and called for the Homicide Unit, and notified Sergeant Henry of the Fifth District."

Both teenagers had been bound with their hands behind their backs. Their legs had been tied together at the ankles, and the mouths of both boys had been "bound with what appears to be a brown terry cloth material…this ligature goes through the mouth and is knotted at the back of the (victims') neck." Richard Stephenson was found lying on his right side, "in an almost fetal-type position." Scott Nelson was found lying face down, "with the right side of his face against the ground."

Back at the Nelson home, the worried parents waited for their child to return from what they hoped was a mere traffic stop, a speeding ticket, or something they could easily correct. They couldn't have known how terrible the next few hours would be or what they would be faced with when Detective Eugene Sherrard, accompanied by Deputy Coroner Carl Adams, came to their home in the wee hours of that Sunday morning to break the terrible news.

The discovery of the bodies of Richard Stephenson and Scott Nelson (both of whom were considered to be good kids from upstanding homes), sent a psychological shock wave reverberating throughout the city of Louisville. Stunned and grief stricken, people kept asking how these boys could have been murdered - execution style - and what kind of a person or persons could have done such an awful thing?

Indeed, the murders sparked an investigation that included almost every available officer on the force. Some of the detectives worked virtually around the clock, grabbing sleep and food whenever and wherever possible. Sergeant Carl Yates, spokesperson for the Louisville Police Department, summed up the intense feelings of the investigators working the case, when he spoke with a reporter for *The Courier-Journal* and said the following: "You think you've seen it all, and seen it many times over. And then you see this. When it comes to young people, lying in the weeds in the middle of the night like that... well, I just can't describe the mood of the officers at the scene."

On Monday morning, *The Courier-Journal* ran the story of the murders on page one, complete with pictures of the slain youth. And soon, police would begin interviewing those who'd spoken with the boys as they sought directions to the Manuel High School stadium only hours before they were killed. When authorities first began their investigation, the only solid information they had was what time the students left home, who was driving, and where they were going. They had no idea whether the boys made it to the game, but it soon became evident from interviews they were conducting with their classmates who did attend, that no one remembered seeing them. And so, accounting for the whereabouts of the two between the hours of 8:00 p.m. when they left home, and 3:05 a.m. when their bodies were discovered, was of utmost importance.

Among those who came forward after seeing pictures of the boys in the newspaper, was an individual who said the students stopped at a store to ask directions sometime between 8:00 and 8:30 p.m. Another witness told detectives that as she waited to catch a bus, the two asked directions from her between 8:30 and 9:00 p.m. And then, in the midst of this intense, city-wide manhunt, came the information that two witnesses had seen the kids being abducted at gunpoint by two African-American males from the *Moby Dick* restaurant, located on the southeast corner of Logan and Oak streets, at about 9 p.m.

By Wednesday evening, October 3, police received information that a George Ellis Wade, 23, and a Victor Dewayne Taylor, 24, were responsible for the kidnapping and murder of Scott Nelson and Richard Stephenson. Apparently, Taylor and Wade were not only talking about the crime, but had carried away items belonging to the dead boys; items that would soon be found by police, giving them what authorities would later describe as overwhelming evidence against the pair.

Both men had extensive criminal records. Between 1978 and 1984, Victor Taylor had been arrested twenty times on a variety of charges, including robbery and assault. Although he was sentenced to thirteen years in prison in 1980, he was paroled to a halfway house in Louisville in 1982. Apparently unconcerned with the ramifications of such an act, Taylor soon left the halfway house and would not be found and rearrested by parole officers for another eight months. Taylor was then returned to prison, but he was released again on June 22, 1984, a little over three months before the murders. George Ellis Wade, also well-acquainted with the justice system, had been arrested fifteen times between 1980 and 1984, for such things as third-degree burglary, shoplifting, and carrying concealed a deadly weapon. He was released from jail only about a month before the Trinity boys were killed.

Louisville Police arrested Wade at 2:20 a.m., October 4. Taylor was picked up two hours later as he was walking down Oak Street. Soon after their separate interrogations began, Wade was informed he'd been positively identified in the line-up as one of the men witnesses had seen abducting the two boys from the restaurant. Upon hearing this, Wade quickly admitted his involvement in the robbery and abduction of the students, but declared Taylor had murdered the boys. As Wade 'sang' like the proverbial canary, Taylor remained silent, refusing to cooperate with authorities. But this didn't concern police, for they were aware that he'd already spoken in great detail about the murders to others. In a taped statement given to police, Wade explained how he and Taylor crossed paths with the doomed students, and what the boys' final moments were like.

According to Wade, the pair walked to *Moby Dick* so Taylor could purchase a fish sandwich. As Wade was waiting outside the restaurant, Scott Nelson, driving the Datsun, pulled up, and Richard Stephenson got out of the car to ask directions. While Stephenson was talking to Wade, Taylor came out and joined in the conversation. Wade told police he and Taylor tried to tell the kids where the stadium was located, and then Taylor asked the boys for a ride, but Stephenson said, no, they couldn't do that. "They wouldn't give us no ride, you know," Wade confessed, "so Vic pulled out the pistol like that. He said 'get in' like that. We got in the back seat." Taylor, pistol in hand, sat behind Nelson, Wade behind Stephenson. Taylor told Nelson to drive north on Logan and to turn left on St. Catherine Street. The four then turned into an alleyway off Clay Street. Here the students were ordered out of the car, robbed, and had their hands tied behind their backs by Wade, as Taylor kept them at gun point. They were then placed in the back seat of Nelson's car.

Wade maintained in his statement that he and Taylor wanted to use the car, and the only way to do that was to completely tie them up and leave them somewhere where they wouldn't be found until much later. The alley off Clay Street, they determined, was the most suitable place to do this. Instead, Wade and Taylor decided to drive the bound youths to a dilapidated area on Ardella Court.

It was perhaps 9:30 p.m. when they turned onto the alleyway known as Ardella Court. After exiting the car, the boys were forced to lie down in the over-grown and weed covered lot. After removing their pants, Wade bound their ankles together and gagged them. It was at this time Taylor and Wade decided not to use the Datsun, and instead, began gathering together all the things they planned on stealing from the boys, and used the pants to wipe any fingerprints off the car.

Wade said that as they were walking away, Taylor began saying the boys had seen their faces, but Wade said that didn't matter, as "they couldn't identify us from any other black person because they was young, plus they wasn't from around here." After this, Wade said, Taylor told him to "hold up a minute." Wade states he told Taylor not to kill the boys, but Taylor went back toward them anyway. After hearing the first shot, he started running down Ardella Court, but before he even reached Waterbury alley (which cuts across Ardella) he heard the second shot. "I knew what it was," he told authorities.

After the murders, the two men walked to Taylor's mother's house at 915 South Jackson Street where a later search by authorities would uncover several items belonging to the two murdered boys. Eugene Taylor, a cousin of Victor Taylor, said he was at the Taylor home playing cards with other members of the Taylor family when Taylor and Wade walked into the house. Eugene Taylor said as they entered the house, "they were smiling, and as I recall, laughing," and they came into the house carrying various personal items, including a Trinity High School gym bag.

Later in the morning of October 4, both men were charged with two counts of kidnapping, two counts of first-degree robbery, two counts of murder, and first degree sodomy. From the start, police believed at least one of the youths had been sodomized although the initial autopsies ruled this out. However, lab results later confirmed one of the boys had been sexually assaulted.

Victor Dewayne Taylor and George Ellis Wade would stand trial in early 1986. Because of the notoriety of the case, they would be granted a change of venue to Lexington, Kentucky, and the pair would be tried separately. While incarcerated in a Lexington jail, Taylor confided in a fellow cellmate who was considered a jail-house lawyer, because he was concerned what Wade's statement might do to him once he had his day in court. Of course, Taylor never expected Ron Smith (a pseudonym) to testify against him, but that is exactly what happened. According to Smith, Taylor admitted to killing the boys because he didn't want them to identify him as being one of the two men responsible for kidnapping and robbing them. Taylor, also, said the students stopped at the restaurant, not to ask directions, but to buy marijuana from them.

But perhaps the most stunning admission came when Taylor told Smith that he and Wade sexually assaulted one of the boys. Wade said this never happened, and was acquitted of this charge during his trial. Franklin Jewell, Victor Taylor's attorney, who understood that Smith would be rewarded (in the form of a reduced sentence), for cooperating with the authorities, verbally blasted Brown in open court, going so far as to compare him to Judas, and what he had down to Christ. This, according to *The Courier-Journal*, "angered and surprised many courtroom spectators."

In the end, Victor Taylor was convicted and sentenced to death for the kidnapping and murder of Scott Nelson and Richard Stephenson, and was convicted on the sodomy charge as well. Today, Taylor remains on death row at the maximum-security prison in Eddyville, Kentucky, more likely to die of old age than be executed. George Ellis Wade was given a life sentence for his role in the killings, and while he is currently eligible for parole, it is highly unlikely he will be released from prison any time soon, and may, in fact, die behind bars. This, of course, would be just fine for the shattered families of Scott Nelson and Richard Stephenson.

Victor Taylor, killer of two teenagers, continues to grow old on Kentucky's death row

The field where Victor Taylor shot and killed Scott Nelson and Richard Stephenson

A Voice From Above

At approximately 2 a.m., on July 6, 2001, forty-four-year-old Monica Berger, a woman with a history of mental illness, walked into the kitchen of her townhouse at 105 Gardiner Lake Road, retrieved a twelve-inch butcher knife from its holder, and began the short walk up the stairs to her son's room. Two-year-old Joey Berger, the adopted son of Gregory and Monica Berger, was sleeping soundly in his room, wearing only a tee-shirt and diaper. A beautiful little boy, little Joey had recently moved with his mother to Louisville from Jasper, Indiana, after she separated from her husband.

As she ascended the steps, she held the butcher knife in her right hand and stared straight ahead. She was confident in her actions and knew exactly what to do, for as she would soon tell others, she'd received her directions directly from God. No one knows if she stood silently for awhile, just watching her son as he slept peacefully, or whether she attacked the moment she entered the room. What is known is that once the stabbing and slicing began, Joey briefly opened his eyes one last time. Death, however, came very quickly, and after taking a last breath, his eyes became fixed and remained open.

Her mission accomplished, Monica Berger dropped the bloody knife and made her way back downstairs, picked up the cordless phone, and dialed 911. The following conversation was taken directly from that call:

"You need police, fire, or EMS?"

"Yes, I just killed my son."

"Stay on the line, ma'am, I'll get you the Louisville Police Department."

"(dial tone dialing) 'I'd do it for my soul. I'd do it for my soul. I'd do it for my soul.

I'd do it for my soul. I'd do it for my soul."

(inaudible)

"I'd do it for my soul."

"I have the 911 transfer, thank you."

"I just killed my son."

The first officer to arrive on the scene was Sergeant Denny Alfred, at 2:15 a.m., followed minutes later by Officer Robert Schroeder, and off-duty Officer Scott Sturgeon. Minutes later, Emergency Medical Services personal arrived, but they were prevented from entering the crime scene until police had secured the area. The first thing police saw was a blood trail on the outside steps leading to the front door, which was standing ajar. Thus far, the only missing component was the distraught woman caller.

As detectives entered the scene they encountered a good deal of blood just inside the doorway. Blood droplets, in a circular fashion, were found in the kitchen, and a blood trail from here led up the stairs: stairs that would soon be ascended by officers Alfred and Schroeder. Reaching the top of the stairs, the officers turned left and entered the room where little Joey Berger was lying in his bed. Believing the child was dead, they called downstairs for the E.M.S. workers, as Detective Jeff Wheeler began examining the body: "The victim is laying in a pool of blood (and) is dressed in a red, blood-soaked shirt with some type of design on the front, and a white diaper in the groin area. The victim has severe trauma to his upper torso with his bowels hanging out, as well as his stomach with food contents showing." Detective Wheeler also noted "the victim's eyes were open." Monica Berger had left the white handled butcher knife lying by her son's left foot.

As there was no sign of the distraught caller confessing to the murder of her son, Schroeder and Alfred returned outside to search for her. Unbeknownst to the pair, however, was that off-duty officer, Robert Gariepy, had located a woman wandering along Gardiner Lane wearing a bloody nightgown and was in the process of returning her to 105 Gardiner Lane. But Monica Berger would not remain at the scene of her crime very long. By 3:18 a.m., she was led into the homicide office of the Louisville Police Department, with the initial interview being conducted by lead investigator Detective Michael Crask.

"Noting the time to be approximately 0328 hours (3:28 a.m.)" he began in his report, "I read to Monica Berger a Consent to Search form, LPD # 0007-96, which is a consent to search…she asked why we needed to search her apartment, and I explained we needed to process the scene for evidence, document evidence, and collect evidence." Upon hearing this, Berger objected, saying, "I think you should get a search warrant." Although obtaining a warrant wouldn't be a problem, he did have a dispatcher radio the team at the Berger residence, telling them to immediately stop their search until a warrant was issued.

Even though the gathering of evidence at the murder scene had to wait, the interrogation by the detective didn't. As Crask broached the subject of Joey's murder, Berger said she was willing to talk about it, but not before she had something to eat. Reaching into his pocket, Crask handed another officer three dollars, instructing him to purchase for "Ms. Berger, a bag of cookies, a bag of chips, and a Sprite" from the vending machines located in the department's basement.

While she waited for her snacks and drink, Monica Berger exchanged the bloody nightgown she'd been wearing for a regulation orange jumpsuit. Because she'd sliced her right index finger while she was killing her son, EMS personal were allowed to enter and place a temporary bandage on the wound.

Needing to document the interview, Crask explained to the strange woman that he could either record their conversation or take notes. Berger said no to a recording, but said notes were fine. When the detective asked if she understood why she'd been brought to his office, she said, "I did it…I killed him, so I could show my soul that I could love again." When Crask asked her directly if she killed her son, Berger responded, "You will never understand, I had to do it for my soul."

"I told Monica Berger" Crask stated in his report, "that I did not understand, but that I wanted to try to understand. I told her I did not know how killing a two-year-old as he slept in his bed, would be something a person would do to save their soul." After sitting silently for a moment, Berger declared, "That's between me and God." As the interview progressed, Berger made it abundantly clear the killing of Joey was carried out not just with the consent of God, but on direct orders from God, emphatically stating, "God told me to kill him." Crask, on the other hand, believing that a more earthly reason might exist for the infanticide, asked Berger if she had murdered her son to get back at her husband. "I don't want to talk about that," was all she would say.

As the homicide investigator started probing into the actual murder with questions like whether or not Joey was sleeping when she stabbed him, she kept her eyes focused on the table and refused to answer right away. But when Detective Crask inquired whether it "bothered her" when she began stabbing Joey, she quickly spoke up, "No. I did it for my soul."

Although most of the interview consisted of the same nonsensical and repeated answers revolving around God and the saving of her soul, at one point she did feel something bad may have happened: "I asked Monica Berger if she thought she should be punished for what she did (but) she would not answer. I then asked if she thought she should go to jail for what she had done to her son. She paused for several minutes…sat on the edge of her chair…looked directly at me (and said) 'I'm ready to go to jail for what I did, I should go to jail, I did it, I'm ready to sign a confession.'" After several minutes, however, she retracted the offer of a signed confession.

At 5:45 a.m., Detective Crask transferred custody of Monica Berger to Homicide Sergeant Pete McCartney, who in turn, by 9 a.m., transported his prisoner to the University of Louisville Hospital several blocks away for treatment of her sliced finger. Evidently, confusion was a major controlling factor in Monica Berger's life at that time, for while she made it clear to investigators she would no longer speak to them without an attorney being present, that rule did not apply to hospital staff. As Berger was being processed for out-patient care, she blurted out she'd killed her son, and she wasn't sorry for doing so. Detective McCartney watched the look of shock spread across the face of Nurse Karen Jensen and quickly apologized for not warning her in advance about the situation. Berger, however, wasn't finished with the tattling. As she sat in an examining room waiting to see a doctor, she spoke with Nurse Michael Hays, who asked her if she wanted a blanket; she said, "No." When he asked her to momentarily get off the bed, so he could change the sheets, she complied, saying, "Please be careful of my finger. I cut myself killing my boy."

"How old was he?" Hayes inquired.

"Two and a half."

"Do you know why you killed your son?"

"To save my soul."

"Who told you that?"

"God," responded Berger, adding that she now has "her self-esteem back...has peace...and knows...he is in Heaven."

Soon after this, Michael Hayes, who was also a minister at a local church, believed he might just be able to help Berger through a spiritual application and introduction to his religious faith. Unfortunately, the psychotic ramblings of Ms. Berger would continue despite his best efforts.

After being treated, Berger was transferred to the Jefferson County Jail. During the short drive over, Berger kept her thoughts to herself. It wasn't until she walked through the main entrance, wherein all prisoners are led, that she said, "I don't want to sign a confession, but I know I've done something bad...I am not crazy."

Be that as it may, Monica Berger would never stand trial for the murder of her son. Four psychiatrists evaluated her, and all four agreed that Monica Berger was criminally insane at the time of the murder, and, as such, she was involuntarily committed to a mental institution in February of 2002. Of course, it is the hope of the medical field that those who enter the system will receive the help they need, and perhaps, at some time in the future, enter society once again as a normal, productive citizen. But in the case of Monica Berger this was not to be. On Monday, May 26, 2003, while on a home visit to her parents' house, she ingested a lethal dose of her anti-psychotic medication. According to an article published in *The Courier-Journal*, as the ambulance raced to the scene, "Berger turned to her father and said 'Dad, it's alright. I just want to be with Joey.'"

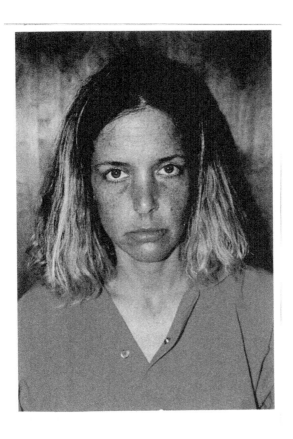

*The mug shot of Monica Berger, only hours after the murder of
her son*

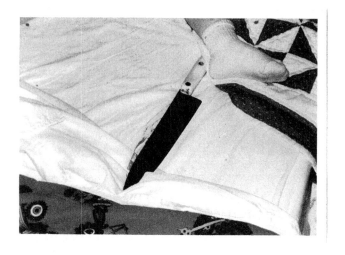

The bloody weapon and the sock-encased foot of young Joey

About The Author

A writer of history and true crime, Kevin M. Sullivan is the author of nine books, a former investigative journalist for both print and online media, and is a recognized authority on serial sex killer, Ted Bundy. Indeed, his "break out" book, *The Bundy Murders: A Comprehensive History*, published by McFarland in 2009, was the catalyst that brought him much attention in the true crime world, leading to numerous radio programs and contacts from documentarians both here in the United States and the United Kingdom. Portions of this work also appear in the college textbook, Abnormal Psychology: Clinical Perspectives on Psychological Disorders, published by McGraw-Hill in November 2012.

Thank you for reading *Kentucy Bloodbath*. Word-of-mouth is crucial to the success of any author. If you enjoyed *Kentucky Bloodbath* then I'd appreciate it if you provided an honest review at http://wildbluepress.com/KentuckyBloodbathReviews.

You can sign up for advance notice of new releases at: http://wildbluepress.com/AdvanceNotice

Thank you for your interest in my books,

Kevin Sullivan

Other WildBlue Press Books
By Kevin Sullivan

VAMPIRE: *The Richard Chase Murders*
http://wbp.bz/vampire

THE TRAIL OF TED BUNDY:
Digging Up The Untold Stories
http://wbp.bz/trailbundy

THE BUNDY SECRETS: *Hidden Files*
On America's Worst Serial Killer
http://wbp.bz/bundysecrets

See even more at:
http://wbp.bz/tc

More True Crime You'll Love From WildBlue Press

BOGEYMAN: He Was Every Parent's Nightmare by Steve Jackson
"A master class in true crime reporting. He writes with both muscle and heart." (Gregg Olsen, New York Time bestselling author). A national true crime bestseller about the efforts of tenacious Texas lawmen to solve the cold case murders of three little girls and hold their killer accountable for his horrific crimes by New York Times bestselling author Steve Jackson. *"Absorbing and haunting!"*(Ron Franscell, national bestselling author and journalist)

wbp.bz/bogeyman

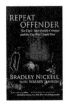

REPEAT OFFENDER by Bradley Nickell
"Best True Crime Book of 2015" (Suspense Magazine) A "Sin City" cop recounts his efforts to catch one of the most prolific criminals to ever walk the neon-lit streets of Las Vegas. *"If you like mayhem, madness, and suspense, Repeat Offender is the book to read."*(Aphrodite Jones, New York Times bestselling author)

wbp.bz/ro

DADDY'S LITTLE SECRET by Denise Wallace
"An engrossing true story." (John Ferak, bestselling author of Failure Of Justice, Body Of Proof, and Dixie's Last Stand) Daddy's Little Secret is the poignant true crime story about a daughter who, upon her father's murder, learns of his secret double-life. She had looked the other way about other hidden facets of his life - deadly secrets that could help his killer escape the death penalty, should she come forward.

wbp.bz/dls

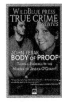

BODY OF PROOF by John Ferak
"A superbly crafted tale of murder and mystery."– (Jim Hollock, author of award-winning BORN TO LOSE) When Jessica O'Grady, a tall, starry-eyed Omaha co-ed, disappeared in May 2006, leaving behind only a blood-stained mattress, her "Mr. Right," Christopher Edwards, became the suspect. Forensic evidence gathered by CSI stalwart Dave Kofoed, a man driven to solve high-profile murders, was used to convict Edwards. But was the evidence tainted? A true crime thriller written by bestselling author and award-winning journalist John Ferak.

wbp.bz/bop

Printed in Great Britain
by Amazon